D1085470

Women in Motion

WOMEN IN MOTION

SANDY HAYDEN
DAPHNE HALL
PAT STUECK

BEACON PRESS
BOSTON

Beacon Press books are published under the auspices
of the Unitarian Universalist Association,
25 Beacon Street, Boston, Massachusetts 02108
Published simultaneously in Canada by
Fitzhenry & Whiteside Limited, Toronto

Printed in the United States of America

(hardcover) 9 8 7 6 5 4 3 2 1
(paperback) 9 8 7 6 5 4 3 2 1

Library of Congress Cataloging in Publication Data
Hayden, Sandy, 1952-
    Women in Motion.

    1. Physical fitness for women.   2. Movement,
Psychology of.   3. Women – Health and hygiene.   I. Hall,
Daphne, 1950–   II. Stueck, Pat, 1945–
III. Title.
GV482.H39 1983   613.7'045   82-70572
ISBN 0-8070-2156-3

Contents

Preface

THIS IS NOT a "Let's do fifty jumping jacks" book. There are no specific exercises to do or charts to follow. No assumptions are made about how fit you are or want to be. What you'll find here instead is yourself – a woman who is active, whether or not she admits it. You'll be taken on a guided tour of being a woman in motion. Each of us adds a different dimension to the book. Together, we offer alternative answers to the question of how women can remain active. The perspective we advocate is easily obtainable.

Sandy is a dedicated physical educator and journalist. Committed to the idea that everyone feels at home as a mover, Sandy relates ways of making the most of each movement experience; she is the originator of the term "selfful experiences." She has taught at the college level and has a respect and understanding for the needs of adults. Drawing from her communications background, Sandy asks you to think twice about how you see yourself in motion and why. Based on her physical education expertise, she gives you a solid base from which to evaluate and act on your movement repertoire.

Daphne picks up from there, detailing many ways a woman is able to move. As a movement education specialist, Daphne translates human movement into understandable terms and examples. You'll discover how much you have taken for granted, and this knowledge will allow you to have a more active role in helping yourself and others. Daphne offers a different vocabulary to express what movement is all about.

Daphne also uses her experiences as a group leader and adventurer to give women a lasting taste of both risk taking and the wilderness. She takes into account, as we all do, that women come in different ages and levels of skill.

Pat rounds out the trio with her background in sports medicine and athletic training. She explodes the myths about physiological reasons for women's inactivity. Having worked with females from kindergarten to adult, Pat has seen how girls and women react to being active. Her information allows you to become knowledgeable about yourself in motion. You'll be confident about placing fewer restrictions on yourself.

Combining athletics with physical education, Pat is well qualified to assess the currently popular health clubs. Her experiences as an employee of a spa make her warnings and suggestions deserving of attention. She supplies a wealth of information that can be used by women to evaluate other organized settings as well.

Throughout the book, we offer support and encouragement. Our belief is that the more knowledgeable and comfortable you are, the more active you will be.

The process of writing this book has involved many people. Bill Stueck kept his wife, Pat, supplied with more moral support than she could have asked for. His encouragement and the energy of friends were a constant reminder that she could successfully complete the task. Having the direct support of all our families and friends can't be overemphasized.

Those influencing us and our ideas are Kate Barrett, George Graham, Norma Jean Harbin, Bill Harper, Margaret Howard, and Judy Jensen. The friends who helped us refine our ideas into words include Ann Clendenin, Estelle Farmer, Trish Hutchinson, Marta Pasternak, and Lori Winter. They read and commented on the many stages of the manuscript with humor, seriousness, venom, accuracy, praise, encouragement, and love.

Extra life has been injected into this book by the many interviews and discussions we had with women. Although fictitious names are used to ensure privacy, the first-person accounts of women in motion add flavor and intimacy.

Pat and Daphne are especially grateful for Sandy's guidance and editing. She was responsible for the initial conception of the book as well as the editing and typing of the chapters in their many revisions. The good qualities of this book are an outgrowth of her vision and her ability to help others express their own.

Two other important sources need to be recognized: physical educators and the staff of Beacon Press. Without physical educators who offer programs that include everyone and without the courage of Beacon Press to publish this unique book, we would have had neither a story to tell nor a means to get it across to the public. An extra thank you goes to MaryAnn Lash and Joanne Wyckoff for editing and prodding this book into shape.

We also thank each other for seeing this project through, and you readers who share an interest and involvement in **women in motion**.

SANDY, DAPHNE, AND PAT
ATHENS, GEORGIA

1
Get Ready for the Possible

A WOMAN in motion. Does it sound like you – or somebody else? Is there a ring of familiarity – or does the idea seem foreign?

Women move. Regardless of the day's events, they are in motion. Turning over in bed to get away from the noise of an alarm clock, jumping onto the curb before a car drives through a crosswalk, tapping fingers or toes while thinking, or sitting and rocking in a chair on the front porch are ways women move daily.

Some women deny they are in motion because they're not participating in athletic contests. To see themselves as movers, such women have to have a lot of external validation. They have to hear a crowd, see a scoreboard, or wear a uniform. They don't notice motion unless it is accompanied by fanfare.

Most of women's movements, however, occur without a dynamic setting. There is no pep band. There are no programs. No one has placed any bets, and the results will not be tomorrow's news. Experiencing movement is a personal affair. Each woman has to determine for herself the importance of how and why she moves. To wait for the crowd and the fanfare to appear is to wait for a moment unlikely to happen.

Many women are already participating in activities that they don't need to initiate; they need only to notice them.

Breaking ground for a garden, vacuuming dog hairs, splitting wood, and walking to work are valuable ways of moving. Running a race and coming in next to last is no less important than coming in first – if you value your own movement experiences and judge yourself fairly.

Women who deny their connections with activity experience discomfort rather than enjoyment. They continually drop, change, or avoid activities, never really knowing why. They've never learned to see themselves as daily movers. No one has shown them that being active doesn't only mean being a skilled athlete in an organized sport. It is possible, however, for all women to learn to see and feel themselves in motion.

"I'm already active," you might think. "There's not much to learn. I already do it." Even if you ski, play racquetball, or lift weights, you may not be making the most of what you're doing. More than likely, you've unintentionally limited yourself to certain activities. Not only can you learn to see in a new light what you're already doing, but you can discover other ways to be active.

Accept that you're in motion. Begin to pay special attention to the variety of movements you make. It doesn't matter if you currently see yourself as athletic, sedentary, or somewhere in between. You can gain more enjoyment and satisfaction from all of your movements by becoming more aware of them. Being in motion is more than playing games. It's a lifetime pursuit.

HOW ACTIVE ARE YOU?

Sometime, somewhere, you determined your threshold of activity and you have given yourself specific doses of movement. Maybe it has been a daily three-mile run, twenty laps in the pool each weekend, or an intense workout when you vacation. You probably have a pattern that you follow.

Even when you are active, however, you may not be aware of how active you are. If you bicycle to work daily, you just consider it part of the job. If your clothes start fitting you better, you applaud the fabric softener. You haven't given yourself the credit; you have seen your own part as inconsequential.

One woman who does this is Holly. When asked if she considered herself to be active, without any hesitation she answered no. When asked what activities she did regularly, Holly said she dances at least three times every week. Brenda also denied being active, but then she said she often played racquetball and practiced yoga.

Ask yourself how you are active. Whether you're a professional athlete or a professional procrastinator, you'll come up with more answers than you thought possible. You probably walk to your favorite spot to eat lunch, wrestle with your children, run up a flight of stairs two steps at a time to keep an appointment, stretch to reach a box of cereal at the back of the shelf, or pull again and again on the cord to get the lawn mower started.

These are ways of being active, but they're different from participating in sports. They're such simple, everyday occurrences, they're overlooked. Holly and Brenda had trouble remembering their activities because they just do them, without much recognition from others – or themselves. But not knowing you're active doesn't mean you're not in motion.

Forget the setting. Don't look at your level of skill. Just watch yourself in motion. Don't let your skill in one activity overshadow how involved you are in another. If you question the amount of your daily movement, think what it would be like to live your life in a space the size of your bedroom. It will quickly become apparent that you're active in many ways that are hard to see.

Often women keep trying to remain active even when they are not sure of success and are forever reminded of how many ways there are to fail. Learning to persevere when success seems impossible is a skill worth pursuing. A woman new to bowling said, "I just took the attitude that I don't care anymore. I'm not going to follow the rules. I'm just going to throw the ball down the center and hope for the best. When I stopped worrying about form, sliding, doing everything just like everybody else and just rolled the ball down the center, I did great."

After playing badminton for the first time, a woman said, "I thought I would not be able to play halfway decently, but I played today and I like it. I think badminton is fun." Another woman "discovered that tennis involves physical ability and endurance as well as strategies. Every game is different as well as every play. I feel I have been taught well and with enthusiasm and this has made me really like tennis."

Being active is more than playing. It's *wanting* to be active. The desire you have to move is important. Seeing yourself as an active female participant requires that you gain control of yourself and face whatever obstacles come between you and that desire. Role models help; a lack of them hurts. It's much easier to see how active you are and to stay in motion when you know someone who has been successful. Your desire and some role models help you become active and remain active. You easily welcome activity into your life. Instead of asking yourself "Am I active?" start with "How am I active?" You'll discover more about yourself more quickly.

Recalling pleasurable experiences can downplay self-consciousness and emphasize the joys of moving. "My parents and brother have always been good tennis players," said one woman, "and they have encouraged me to learn also. I've always wanted to know how but have never taken the time to excel at it. Now that I've learned the proper way to play, there is no use in stopping there. I want to become good at tennis."

Other women cited their own reasons for becoming active tennis players:

- "My brother has always played tennis and I decided it would be fun to learn how, so someday I can say 'yes' when he wants me to play with him."

- "My mother needs someone in the family to play tennis with."
- "My boyfriend plays often and has been begging me to learn how to play."
- "I need some kind of activity and I think tennis could be the game I'm looking for."
- "I enjoy watching and would like to play tennis without embarrassing myself."

The contact women have with other people and the degree of encouragement other people offer influence women's willingness to take their activity seriously.

Even with desire and encouragement, women must search harder for coplayers as the years go by. "I've gotten more involved in individual sports," said Darlene, "because I'm getting older and it's getting more difficult to find the numbers you need for a team sport. Also, I have a better self-concept now. I was always self-conscious because I was a chunky kid. So I did team sports where I wasn't a central figure."

Emily echoed these sentiments. "When I was active before, it was more on a group basis, and now what I do is more on an individual basis. I don't want to be on a schedule with scheduled games. I enjoy just playing golf or a game of tennis." Emily has been trying other new activities as well. "I just bought a sailboat," she said, "and I'm not a swimmer. I can swim, but I have a fear of the water. So buying the sailboat is a kind of risk and challenge. I'm not really scared. I'm excited. I thought it would be a nicer, more peaceful thing to do on weekends than drive somewhere and camp."

Several years ago, Emily took advantage of nearby mountains and taught herself how to ski. "That's the way I've learned," she said. "Just going out and falling. Over a four-year period, I improved a lot. It was a challenge."

Emily hasn't always led an active life. A change in employment affected her active lifestyle. "I went through an inactive period," Emily said, "when I got out of teaching and got a sit-down job." After moving to another location, she found herself back among active people. "Only with the influence of others being active," she noted, "have I started being active again."

Even if finding teammates is more difficult for women as they get older, other activities are in reach – like weightlifting. "I just increased my maximum on the bench press," Carson said. "It was exciting. I decided to try it, and I did a twenty-pound increase. I was testing my potential. I knew in the future that I could. I'm getting stronger. I'm changing. Strength equals power. The body can always get stronger. I know it's possible – self-testing and all. It's personal and psychological strength as well as physical." She has enjoyed getting to know her body's strength and feeling healthier. "I was so weak. I never used these muscles. Now I can lift couches."

Carson's motivation is bolstered by her attitude that she'll "try anything once. It comes from a basic desire to be active. I don't lack confidence in trying. My father's an athlete and always wanted us to be active. I always admired those kinds of people."

PERSONAL FITNESS

You may admire a woman who can move furniture with ease, hit a softball deep into the outfield, artistically perform a modern dance, or climb vertical rock faces. Expecting yourself to accomplish such feats may not be reasonable. You may have no need or desire to do anything more than play volleyball once a week with your friends. Admiration doesn't have to lead to imitation. You're not obligated to be a superwoman, unless you truly want to be.

Women can be physically fit in many ways. But the most common way to judge fitness is by the way a woman looks. Women judge and are judged by bodily appearance. There is no absolute standard, however: long-distance runners tend to be thinner than the norm, and some women need more body mass for the activities they do. Taking measurements of the percentage of body fat, how much oxygen a woman uses, the distance she covers in a certain time, or resting and active pulse rates help determine a woman's level of fitness.

Often what is left out, however, is how a woman feels – as her own judge of fitness. Being fit according to clinical standards does not necessarily mesh with one's own standards. An awareness of both types of fitness is needed to enjoy total fitness. It's up to each woman to combine physiological determinants of fitness with personal expectations and desires.

Making your own decisions, rather than following established guidelines, personalizes activity. Decide what you like about movement and take responsibility for keeping yourself satisfied. Why do forty laps around a track when you don't enjoy it? If you recognize what activity is right for you, you have a better chance of staying active. Each person has her own unique method of staying fit. Following someone else's plan is a sure way of leaving some of your own needs unsatisfied. Pay attention to yourself, discover what you enjoy doing, and take control of what you do.

"I like the way I am when I'm active," said Darlene. "I think it's fun. I like to feel my muscles contract and relax. It's aesthetically pleasing. I like the losing and gaining of equilibrium and pushing myself and seeing how far I can go. I don't like to jog or run, but I like to run on a basketball or tennis court. I hate to run unless it's part of a game. I think I enjoy sprinting more than I enjoy running. I like the feeling of wind going through my hair and against my skin."

The main reason Emily is active is "my knowledge that it's good for me and makes me feel a lot better. It's invigorating, a release of tension. After I do it, I feel I can do more."

Fran said, "I think everyone needs to do the most they can with what they've got, and that includes the body. In any activity, or in life, the more senses you use the better you feel."

In movement activities, a kinesthetic sense can aid in self-evaluation. That is, a sense of how and what your body feels like when you are in motion is critical to gaining confidence and insight as a mover. Serving in tennis may be difficult for you because when the racket head goes out of sight so do your perceptions of where the racket will be when your arm straightens out to contact the ball. Walking on a creek bed may come easily, however, because you instantly adjust to any imbalance you feel underfoot. Walking a nature trail may not pose any problems, but donning a backpack and walking the trail may make you feel totally off balance and unable to judge how low to stoop to avoid overhanging limbs.

Personal fitness includes your decision about how you would like to make use of your kinesthetic awareness. Your feeling that you don't like to play racquetball may indicate that you're uncomfortable having to listen for the ball when you're used to seeing it in other games. Your avoidance of swimming may be an indirect way of expressing your dislike for having to use your arms and legs and continually to be aware of how they are performing. Each person can process only so much information in the course of an activity. Begin to recognize what makes you feel overloaded and under-loaded.

When you're active, you get feedback. You hit or miss the target, perform efficiently or with exhausting effort, and feel comfortable or awkward. Use these cues. If you want to be more accurate, efficient, and comfortable, be kinesthetically aware. Notice why you do what you do so you can make adjustments. Rationally look at how it feels to be in motion.

In whatever way you choose to be fit, know you can change your expectations as you continue to be active. Fitness isn't absolute. It's relative to what you need and can do at the moment. Be fair and honest with yourself. Don't make yourself believe you must perform a certain way. Give yourself room to experiment. No one else is fit in exactly the same way you are.

FEARS AND EXCUSES

Fear of personal failure and embarrassment keeps some women from being active. They see no worth in moving, and they prevent themselves from moving in such a way that they can see the worth. Their assumption is that they can't fail if they don't do certain activities. Such reasoning is akin to not finding a job because you might be fired – anticipating the worst without taking other likelihoods into account.

Avoidance of physical pain and the possibility of not being tall enough, quick enough, agile enough, strong enough, or young enough can put a deepfreeze on moving too. Such thinking usually doesn't take into account the actual odds of feeling pain or whether the activity calls for height, speed, agility, or any other special talent. The stereotyped perception is that activity does require those things, so why pursue it?

Developing an understanding of yourself as a mover puts fears and concerns in perspective. You can selectively avoid an activity based on information about it rather than on stereotypes. Faced with an unfamiliar activity or situation, women can easily fall back on excuses. When reasoning fails and fears creep in, excuses abound.

There's a fine line between reasons and excuses. Maybe you can identify yourself in these statements and recognize similar remarks you have made as a rationale for not engaging in certain activities:

- It just doesn't fit my personality
- I don't have the time
- It costs too much
- I'm not in shape
- That's for someone younger than me
- My family would never approve
- There's no place to do it in my neighborhood
- I wouldn't know where to begin

If you have been avoiding a certain activity because you have convinced yourself it's out of reach for any reason, test yourself. If you acquired $1,000, would you invest some of it to be able to be more active? If a week-long vacation appeared out of nowhere, would you take the time to play?

If your own reason for avoiding movement activities no longer existed, would you really be more active, or are you just kidding yourself? Have you been giving yourself reasons, or have they turned out to be excuses?

Allow yourself to confront your fears and misconceptions. Be fair to yourself. Look at your movement experiences. Examine the kinds of movements and activities you like best.

Women who know the value of movement activities need to support one another and feel good and right in being active. Support means encouraging yourself and other women without being unduly critical. Pointing out the good and pleasing moments is much more beneficial than pointing out someone's weak points. Appreciating the wonders of a girl who is playing is much more supportive than telling her she acts like a tomboy. Going to intercollegiate athletic events or the neighborhood recreation league to watch women in action is very supportive of the continued growth of all levels and ages of active females.

Providing encouragement is very important because double standards exist for men and women. You can see the stereotypic view of active women in your own attitudes: Do you shy away from movement because someone may notice your muscles developing; your effort shown by perspiration; your desire to contact another player; or your pleasure in moving? Women are just finding out that they're born with the same right to move as men have.

If you consider yourself an athlete or sportswoman, if you have been called a tomboy or have been told you throw or have muscles like a boy, you may have felt defensive. Double standards can make you feel like you're trespassing when you know you're not. To avoid uncertainty women need to take a look at their approaches to movement activities to learn how involved they are and how involved they want to and can be. Sorting out the fears from the excuses helps.

A woman who is comfortable with herself as an active participant may still run the risk of being taunted and teased by people who do not accept the natural sight of women in motion. The woman who is unsure of herself as a mover is even more threatened by comments from unsympathetic outsiders. People who understand the meaning and importance of movement for women offer encouragement, while those who don't understand may offer verbal abuse.

Part of the harassment that comes with double standards is labeling. Someone, somewhere, is going to claim that women who enjoy moving are acting like men, tomboys, and lesbians. The closer women come to recognizing their desires and developing their skills and strengths, the greater the chance they will be subjected to name-calling. Activities that are acceptable for men are deemed unsuitable for women.

This is not to say that women who are active are never gay or don't perform the same motions men do. But movement activities will not cause a change in your own identity. As often as you have eaten foods from different countries, has your nationality changed? There is no reason to accept the falsehood that if you enjoy activities that have been in the male domain you will no longer be an acceptable female. The man or woman who is sure of himself or herself will not deny you the right to be yourself.

A woman's fear of being unfavorably labeled has its origins in the fact that movement activities, especially sports and athletics, have been considered men's territory. Regardless of the history of a particular sport, the current rules and equipment reveal an assumption of a large physique. Some women have such a physique, but most do not.

Sports have been man-tailored. It has taken courage and perseverance from each woman to attempt to master activities in which equipment and rules have thwarted women's involvement. In basketball, the basket is quite high and the ball is large. The grip on tennis rackets has only recently been made to fit a smaller hand. Good running shoes have become available in women's sizes only in the past few years. It wasn't very long ago that dresses, corsets, and restrictive garments were the vogue for women athletes. If bloomers hadn't been invented, who knows how inactive women would still be. Developing speed, agility, and confidence is nearly impossible when you are tied inside tight garments, must wear shoes with heels, and are not expected to perspire.

In the past, and in the present, women have had to adjust their activity because of double standards. The clothing industry has begun to recognize that women can be a large share of the sporting goods market. Athletic bras, shorts, and tops that fit an active woman, running shoes made for women's narrower feet, and other articles of clothing are now available. A woman no longer has to purchase a pair of men's athletic shoes to be sure the sole or upper won't wear out prematurely.

With these products being manufactured to dress the active woman, one concern generally has been overlooked – women come in different shapes and desires. Hips, waists, buttocks, and shoulders have different dimensions on different women. All women who are active aren't slender and of average height, nor would they all choose to be this way. The fit of athletic clothing can encourage or discourage the most faithful movers.

This is not meant to dampen your spirits. If you become more aware of what factors are involved in your decisions about activity, you can influence manufacturers and friends to take your needs more seriously. Given the current economic system, if a true need is uncovered that will likely yield a profit, a product will be made. Use this to your advantage. Vocalize your needs and concerns for athletic wear. Influence next year's line of clothing.

When you've become proficient at spelling out your apparel needs, take a look at the equipment you use and the sports rules and regulations that you follow. If they're suited to you, be pleased. If they're not, do what you can to make changes. Standards can be changed. Equipment can be redesigned and rules amended. There's a lot of room for women to grow in. Many of women's reasons for their inactivity can be linked to inappropriate clothing, equipment, and rules, and changes can lead to more satisfying activity for many women.

In addition to misconceptions about active women's needs, many women have preconceptions about what value certain activities offer them. Statements like "I don't like soccer" or "Football is a male sport" leave little room for recognizing the potential for worthwhile experiences in almost any activity. Such thinking blocks off many options even before they have been explored.

To achieve a better understanding of the variations among movement activities, women need to look at the experiences they have within their activities. Don't hold back from experimenting because something *might* happen. Go out and see for yourself what the activity or movement is really like. The actual situation will likely be more varied and not as absolutely defined as you had imagined.

Women who accept that movement activities are sex-segregated are likely to identify with smooth, rounded, flowing movements and to avoid performing quickly with strong, sharp, distinct actions. Hang-gliding with its need for sharp, quick, linear movements wouldn't be appealing to them, but performing flowing movements on the uneven parallel bars would seem all right.

Both kinds of movement involve risk and challenge. If you look closely, you may be shocked to discover the strength and prowess needed to perform so-called women's sports. Such requirements have always been there, but have been downplayed.

Herding women into specific kinds of movement prevents both an awareness of what women can do and a recognition of the skills women already possess. Expectations are limited. If women perform only the activities specified by a double standard, they may be missing out on an untapped part of their lives.

REWARDS

If you complete your work early one day and are able to take an afternoon off, or if you finish stripping a table or doing another task sooner than expected, how do you congratulate yourself? What do you reward yourself with? Television, the movies, a fast-reading novel, or a social visit may be in order. It may not occur to you to engage in your favorite movement activity. Readjusting your reward system to encourage your activity takes a conscious effort.

Activity can be as much of a treat as reading a book. Developing more regular movement activity can be accomplished by keeping movement on your list of self-rewards. Fun, fitness, socializing, coping with anxiety and stress, and experiencing freedom go along with being in motion. Movement shouldn't be something you do because nothing else comes to mind. Staying active is an important desire. Reward yourself with it more often.

Women in motion are becoming less and less rare. Women are learning to see through double standards and be proud of their desire and willingness to be active. Realizing that you can and will deal with reasons and excuses is another step toward knowing that movement activities offer possibilities that are both meaningful and acceptable.

To acquire a clearer understanding of the struggles and pleasures experienced and yet to be explored, women have to look at themselves attentively. There's a lot to uncover if they make the effort.

By seeing herself as an integrated whole, a woman can begin to notice how movement activities justify themselves. Moving is pleasurable. Moving occurs daily. It happens with and without conscious effort. It doesn't have to yield physical fitness or mental stimulation, but it can. Other people can be close by or nowhere in sight. There may be rules and boundary lines or simply spontaneous actions. The joys of moving *are* known. Women can know them—if they're fair and honest with themselves.

2
Your Movement History

WE ALL HAVE endless memories of movement from childhood through adulthood. Rolling faster and faster to the bottom of the hill. Pumping the swing higher and higher. Plunging from the diving board into the water. Jumping awkwardly from rock to rock. Running breathlessly to catch a fleeing opponent. Cooling tired feet in an icy mountain stream. Even before the earliest of these memories, the importance of movement was established.

Any pregnant woman can vouch for the movement of her baby before its birth. After birth, the newborn continues to be a constant study of kicking, grasping, flexing, and grimacing, even when asleep. As these motions become more controlled and purposeful, moving is the baby's main tool for learning. It provides the direct sensations she needs to experience her immediate environment, eventually enabling her to explore more and more of the world.

A baby who is crawling under her own power is a determined creature. She doesn't want to be held back, put in her playpen, or stopped by having a door closed in her face. As she grows older, she joyfully exhibits her growing sense of independence and curiosity by exploring everything within reach, as well as some things thought to be out of reach.

A toddler once followed her father up a ladder to the roof of the house. He didn't know she had followed him until he looked up from the gutter he was cleaning and saw her starting down the sloped roof toward him. He was shocked. She was merely curious – and determined to go and see what he was doing.

The joy and determination children display when they are moving reveal its importance. For many girls, however, the pattern is to become increasingly less active as they mature into women. That doesn't have to happen. If this has been your pattern, you can change it.

Reach back to your memories of a more active girlhood to bring more meaning and enjoyment to your life. Retrieve information about the past that will help and inspire you to make decisions about your present and future movement activities. Past movement choices and preferences have a definite impact on present habits and attitudes. Increase your current awareness of yourself in motion. Learn to identify skills, patterns, and rhythms that feel right to you. Looking at your movement history is a rich source of self-knowledge.

A PLAYFUL CHILDHOOD

When you were younger, you probably spent a lot of time playing at home, at school, in a park, or in the street. Wherever you played, you probably had no trouble finding plenty of interesting things to do. It's likely that you often didn't want to answer the call to come home for dinner or bedtime.

One woman's favorite childhood activity was using her backyard swing set. She remembers spending hours there in her preschool years, climbing on the bars and swinging. She felt power and rhythm as she pumped to make the swing go higher and higher. At times she would swing and sing, getting higher and louder with every arc.

You can probably remember many play activities that you enjoyed. Thinking back to them can remind you of all the things you used to do. By examining them more closely, you can gain insights into your adult preferences. Make a list of activities you did at home, in the park, on the playground, at school, in physical education class, on vacation, at camp, on teams, and elsewhere. Put a mark to the left of each activity you experienced during childhood. At the end of the list, add as many other active pastimes as you can think of. Identify four or five of your favorite activities. Indicate them with a circle around your original mark. Now go back through your list and put a mark to the right of each activity you've done as an adult. Add activities at the end if necessary. You will use this list of favorite activities to take a closer look at your movement preferences. The accompanying sample list may help jog your memory for making your own list.

I . . .	*and I played . . .*
__ bicycled __	__ badminton __
__ camped out __	__ basketball __
__ climbed trees __	__ boxball __
__ danced __	__ cops and robbers __
__ did gymnastics __	__ croquet __
__ hiked __	__ dodge ball __
__ jogged __	__ football __
__ jumped __	__ handball __
__ paddled __	__ hide and seek __
__ raced __	__ hit the penny __
__ ran __	__ hockey __
__ rode horses __	__ hopscotch __
__ rowed __	__ jacks __
__ sailed __	__ kickball __
__ skated __	__ kick the can __
__ skied __	__ on swings or seesaws __
__ sledded __	__ paddleball __
__ square danced __	__ soccer __
__ swam __	__ softball __
__ tobogganed __	__ tag __
__ tumbled __	__ tennis __
__ walked __	__ tetherball __
__ water skied __	__ volleyball __

FINDING COMMON THREADS

As you consider your favorite activities, look for common elements. The environment is one such thread, as are equipment, focus, pace, and rhythm. People, weather, play areas, and surfaces are all part of the movement environment. The number of people that can participate in an activity at once is a significant feature of an activity, as is the manner of participation. In a swimming pool or exercise room there may be many people moving, but they are not required to have more than fleeting contact with each other. On a team there are also many people, but they cannot choose to ignore the others. Camaraderie is sometimes very intense.

Some activities – such as tennis, backpacking, and golf – need only a few people for participation. The people involved may be partners, opponents, or neither. Your preferred activities on your list may indicate both the number of people you like to have around when you're moving and the degree and types of interaction you prefer.

Many activities are dependent on specific weather conditions. Alpine skiing and sledding require snow. Water skiers prefer warm weather. Spelunkers usually don't care whether it rains. Your favorite childhood activities probably reflect the climate you lived in.

The type of area available for active play and its surface affect movement choices. A woman who has grown up accustomed to the paved surfaces of the city may be somewhat uncomfortable walking on mountain trails that have mud, leaves, loose rocks, or acorns underfoot. A woman who grew up roaming fields and forests may feel too confined when participating in indoor movement activities. Certain types of activity are stimulated by permanent and semipermanent objects in the area, such as trees, stairs, jungle gyms, creeks, ponds, oceans, hills, tetherball poles, basketball goals, goal posts, backstops, and fences.

A woman's environment is often something she takes for granted and learns to exist within and adjust herself to. But it is possible to create an environment and equip it to support your movement preferences, so that you are not manipulated by the environment. A woman who enjoys working and interacting with a team may not be successful when she tries an individual jogging program rather than a team sport. A cross-country ski enthusiast in the deep South will need to alter her environmental preferences and find activities that don't require snow. A country woman in the city may have a special need to seek out parks and gardens for recreation — or even to move back to the country if she can't adjust to the city environment.

Another way to look for similarities among your favorite activities is to consider the kind of equipment used. A woman who lists golf, field hockey, and softball might conclude that she enjoys activities that involve striking balls with long-handled implements. A list that includes gymnastics and diving might reveal a special liking for activities that involve a springy surface for takeoff. Someone who lists cross-country skiing, bicycling, and canoeing as favorite pastimes probably enjoys traveling in a self-propelled manner.

Your favorite activities may have a common thread in their focus, which refers to what you pay attention to as you move. You may pay attention to how your arms stroke the water, to the position of your head, to the sensation of dryness in your throat, to your feelings of well-being and peace, or to your attempts at expression through dance. You might focus externally on where the ball went or should have gone when you hit it, which teammate is open for a pass, where to land on the diving board when preparing for a dive, the beauty of the scenery, the steepness of the trail, or the phrase of music that signals your entrance to the stage.

All activities have a variety of focus elements, but each activity has more of one focus than another. Team games such as basketball and field hockey, for instance, have more external focus than activities that don't involve relationships with other people and objects. In addition, in the same activity two people may concentrate very differently on the same focus or on different focuses. One cyclist may be highly aware of the strength of her legs and how sweaty her head feels under her helmet, while another may be more aware of passing motorists and the scenic neighborhood.

It's important for each woman to know that she is in control of her focus. This helps her enjoy an activity more. Concentrating on scenery or music while pedaling into a stiff head wind might make the ride seem less exhausting without taking away from the efficiency of the pedaling. If the internal focus on bending one's knees is not helping to improve a forehand in tennis, perhaps the external focus on hitting a certain spot on the court will produce better results.

The pace a woman chooses and whether she changes her pace during an activity are highly personal matters. A woman may vary her activities in terms of the pace involved. Her awareness of the pace of her favorite activities and her own preferences can help a woman make decisions about taking up new activities.

Bicycling provides examples of fluctuating pace. During a race of, say, thirty miles, cyclists must ride many laps on a course. As an incentive to the competitors, race sponsors often offer special prizes to the winners of certain laps, encouraging the cyclists to put on bursts of speed. Even those who have no hope of winning the lap push themselves to speed up. When the lap is finished, the racers slow down to their previous speeds, thus demonstrating a fluctuating pace. Women who cycle for recreation also change their pace, sometimes coasting and sometimes pedaling hard. Pacing is one of the joys of bicycling.

In running, a slow, continuous pace does not appeal to everyone. One woman we know doesn't care for this plodding, as she calls it, so she races by alternating periods of fast running and walking. Even though many runners would never walk in a race, she maintains her self-designed leapfrog style because she knows she is happier and more comfortable that way.

Different activities offer a variety of pacing patterns, some having more room for variation than others. One runner prefers a pace she can maintain from start to finish. She likes something about the steady speed and the reward of rest at the end. When she runs with her friend who uses a fluctuating pace, however, she matches her pace to her friend's, changing her usual internal focus to the external one of enjoying her friend's company. Strangely enough, by running at a pace different from her usual one, she has become even more sensitive to her own pacing. She says it has been both helpful and enjoyable to experiment with change.

Most activities have at least a little fluctuation of pace. A dance or floor exercise routine would not be interesting without it. As you look at your favorite activities, try to figure out what the pacing is like. You may notice that the action moves along at the same tempo for a long time and then changes, or that it switches back and forth frequently. There probably are times when you prefer one activity to another simply because of the pacing.

Rhythm is another factor in your individual movement style. Rhythm can be even or uneven, repetitious or varied, simple or complex. Accented movements or gestures may be predictable and regular, or they may come at surprising times, adding a syncopated nature to the activity.

Competitive sports and games are characterized by sudden, unexpected movements that occur when players try to catch each other off guard. Folk dances and individual activities such as running or swimming usually have a repetitious, regular rhythm. Modern dance and the martial arts usually have varied, complex, and syncopated rhythmic patterns. Disco dancing has a heavy and even underlying beat.

A woman's particular choices of elements in her activities make her movement profile unique. Even women we interviewed from the same softball team varied widely in their reasons for playing. The feeling of the bat hitting the ball was one woman's favorite part of the game. Another person liked executing skills as an individual and combining them with team skills. Winning was mentioned as a motivating factor, as well as the recognition received for playing well.

Paying attention to specific aspects of environment, equipment, focus, pace, and rhythm can help women make better choices when they engage in or change movement activities.

There are times when an injury may prohibit participation in some activities but not others. Choosing the right ones is important. Movement activities are important if women want to feel at home in an old or new environment.

NAMES ARE MISLEADING

Identifying activities by their names, such as basketball, square dancing, or swimming, is useful. Names provide convenient handles for distinguishing among activities. The convenience also has disadvantages, however. Names can carry predetermined and stereotyped views of what activities are like and what kinds of people engage in them. You may have missed out on an activity that would have been perfect for you because your impression of the activity was distorted.

Basketball, for instance, brings to mind tall, lean players jumping effortlessly to shoot the ball in the basket. If you were not tall, you may not have been encouraged to play basketball. If your family did not believe girls should play team sports, you may never have had a chance to find out whether you liked them. Many women miss out on participation in enjoyable movement because of such predetermined ideas. Basketball, for instance, has many components besides jumping for the basket. If your analysis of your favorite activities shows that you like team sports and indoor activities with running, varied rhythms, and quick changes of pace, then even if you are not tall, basketball is an activity you might enjoy.

The compartmentalizing and labeling of movement also limits women's thinking to those activities that already have names. It's hard to imagine new and original games, or even variations of old ones, when competitive baseball, football, and basketball receive so much attention and are so well defined.

Many women try to mold themselves to activities this way. They join teams, health clubs, or dance classes, and if they begin to feel unhappy or uncomfortable they assume it's their

fault. They feel there's something wrong with them if they don't enjoy the activity enough to keep doing it.

Emphasizing only activities that have names can prevent a total view of human movement potential and enjoyment. The present culture is so locked into traditional sports and games and how they are "supposed" to be played (that is, to win) that there is very little room for sampling activities without committing oneself to six months of preseason practice and league play. Even if a woman is willing to make a long-term commitment, there is no room for mistakes. Beginners are not welcome. One is supposed to fit the activity instead of molding activities to fit oneself.

Everyone feels awkward sometimes. Some awkward feelings are part of learning a skill or activity. It takes time to adjust to new combinations of movements and to be comfortable with them. It's not fair to expect to be smooth and skillful all the time. Keeping an open mind about movement activities and not feeling bound to do only well-defined and labeled activities create freedom and fun for all.

WORKING WITH CHOICES

Childhood feelings about movement influence women as adults. Ten-year-old Caren, for example, is a friend of everyone in her neighborhood. She enjoys playing with other children as long as she can keep up with them, and she does not like playing alone. Being overweight and not very agile slows her down. This often keeps her on the fringes of any games in which teams are chosen, and she sometimes resents it. But she is very good at activities that don't require speed or agility. She excels at hitting a softball and at swimming, but she doesn't always get a chance to show it or to make the most of her skills.

As an adult, Caren will probably be happiest in team games or in activities that involve other people. She will need to be aware of her strengths and special skills and to choose activities that use her skills. Engaging in an individual strength-

training program, for instance, might lead to failure because of a lack of support rather than a lack of ability.

Unlike Caren, ten-year-old Kelly rarely strays far from home in search of playmates. Much of her time is spent making her bedroom into a castle or the front porch into a stage. She is constantly directing her friends or stuffed animals in acting out one of the many stories she has read. It doesn't really matter to her if anyone else is there. If her friends won't play with her, she takes all the parts herself, seeming to live in a world of her own. A rainy day provides her with wonderful hours for reading, daydreaming, and making up her own stories. During recess at school, she enjoys talking with her friends while she's playing hopscotch or using the swings. She enjoys these kinds of slow-moving, smoothly flowing activities; vigorous activity just doesn't appeal to her.

As she grows older, Kelly will probably have little use for team games or activities. She may not enjoy sports that require running or endurance, such as soccer or basketball. Her sense of flow and drama might be well used in gymnastics or dance. She might find the self-paced rhythms of backpacking or cross-country skiing enjoyable.

Each woman has the experiences of a different little girl in her past. Women remember such varied experiences as eagerly running out of the classroom for recess, avoiding games where teams were chosen for fear of being chosen last, looking in the mirror and being pleased with the reflection, running fast for the sheer pleasure of it, or trying to learn to do something and being ridiculed for not succeeding.

Even negative or painful childhood memories provide important knowledge. They may help explain a woman's aversion to certain movements or provide a challenging learning situation. Most of all, they may show how to avoid situations that cause feelings of isolation and failure. If try-outs and picking teams are sources of pain, then organizing so that everyone can play and making the selection process fair can help girls and women feel more comfortable with movement activities.

MOVEMENT COMPONENTS

Another way to learn more about and expand your movement preferences and possibilities is to consider the movement components of activity. You can learn more from considering these components than you can from looking at only the activities themselves. Components are sometimes described by reference to the body and body parts, but remember that when you move, *all* of you is in motion, including your feelings and ideas.

Movement components may be divided into four areas:

- Movements of your body and body parts—what you move
- Use of the space you are moving in—where you move
- Relationships you have with other objects or with other people—who or what you move with
- Effort qualities of your movement—how you move

These components work together, they are all present at the same time, and they are totally independent of the overall movement activity. When you sweep the sidewalk, walk through a crowded subway station, or throw a Frisbee, you incorporate all the components of movement. This integrated view of movement is a way of looking at all movement without assigning misleading labels.*

WHAT YOU MOVE

Remain seated where you are and see how many ways you can move your arm from the elbow down. Bend your arm, fingers, wrist, and hand. Stretch out those same parts. What part can twist? Bending, stretching, and twisting are the

---

*These movement components were first advanced by Rudolf Laban and have been used to study and describe human movement in situations ranging from factory assembly lines and walking down the street to modern dance and ballet. Many elementary school physical education teachers in the United States use them in movement education. The terms and their meanings are discussed in many texts, but our primary source is Sheila Stanley's book *Physical Education: A Movement Orientation* (Toronto: McGraw-Hill, 1969).

only three actions the body can use to effect movement. These three actions, combined by all the different body parts working together, produce a surprising array of movement patterns.

Think about the activity of getting dressed and try to determine how many different body parts must bend, stretch, and twist. A woman's overall movement preferences often revolve around which body parts she is most comfortable bending, stretching, and twisting. Although a woman's whole body is usually involved in any movement, some parts are momentarily emphasized over others.

There are three ways that body parts get special attention: their use for gestures, as in the moving arms of a folk dancer; their role in leading the action, as in the hands of a diver; and their support of the body's weight, as in crawling. Look at your list of favorite activities. Which body parts are emphasized in each activity? Is there a common thread? If so, do the body parts bear weight, gesture, or lead the action?

Dorian's favorite activities stress her feet and legs, as in running (weight bearing) and kicking (gesturing) to play speedball, squatting (weight bearing) as catcher in softball, and supporting her weight while rock climbing. Women who engage in racket sports would find emphasis on feet and legs for bearing their weight and on the arms for swinging the rackets (gesturing).

When you move your arm from the elbow down, you are moving only part of your body, but often your whole body is involved in a movement. Beginning from a sitting position, what movements would you make if:

- you saw hundred-dollar bills raining outside your window?
- six inches of glue were under your chair?
- a blinding flash of light appeared six feet in front of you?
- a poisonous snake crawled over your foot, seemingly unaware that you were there?

Your responses to the imaginary situations constitute the four types of movements that can be done by the whole body. In the first instance, whether you walked, ran, or sprinted, some form of locomotion would have taken you outside to see where the money was falling from. In the second example, you would jump up on the seat of your chair or another safe height to get away from the glue. In the situation of the flash, turning, whether in avoidance or simply to change your direction, would be a useful action. You could do it in place or while moving. Finally, holding your body in perfect stillness to avoid the snake probably would take more effort than any of the previous three actions. A deliberately held stillness is one of the most all-encompassing actions that you can do.

Which kinds of movement do your favorite activities require: locomotion, elevation, turning, or stillness? How about movement activities that you dislike? When you identify what movements you don't like, you may be able to modify some activities so that those movements are less important. A person who wants to play soccer but doesn't like running may find enjoyment and success at the goalie position.

If you have trouble executing a certain type of movement, learning how to do it may lead to enjoyment instead of displeasure. In racquetball, for instance, it is important to be able to stop and turn quickly and to move in different directions – forward, backward, and sideways. If a woman has not learned to do this, she may be uncomfortable with the abruptly changing nature of the game. Learning how to stop suddenly and pivot and step in any direction could make a previously confusing game enjoyable.

The shape a body takes during a movement usually affects the efficiency of the movement. What word would you use to describe the shape a woman's body takes during the gliding phase of the breast stroke? A common term for that is pin-shaped. A woman might find her body in a flattened-wall shape when she plays goalie in a soccer game. Reaching into the back seat of a car from the front causes the body to assume a spiral shape. Tucking both knees into the chest during a dive puts the body in a rounded shape. In your movements you will notice that your body takes on combinations of shapes or that one part of your body may have one shape while a different part has another.

Imagine you are doing one of your favorite movement activities. Is your whole body involved? If so, are you traveling from one place to another, jumping, or holding yourself perfectly still? Which body parts are accented, and how? Are they gesturing, bearing weight, or leading your action? How would you describe the shape of your body? Does your shape change as you move?

Increasing your awareness of these components of movement can help you understand why some activities are more appealing to you than others. You might also become more efficient in your movement if you can learn to feel the parts of movements that don't fit well with others. Uncurling too soon from the rounded position in the dive would throw off a diver's entry into the water. Taking weight on the wrong foot during a folk dance disturbs the balance and rhythm of the dance. A fuller awareness of how all the movements can combine perfectly enhances the enjoyment of movement.

WHERE YOU MOVE

As an experiment, stand in the middle of the room. While continuing to face in one direction, walk in as many different directions as you can. Try forward, backward, left, and right. Also try diagonal movements. Moving up and down are also possible directions. Your ability to move in different directions is one aspect of spatial awareness.

The path you take to get from one place to another, on the ground, in the air, or in water, is another part of your spatial awareness. The simplest path you could take to get from where you are to a point twenty feet away would be a straight line. The term *zigzag* describes the path you would take while skiing a slalom course. That differs from the path you would make as you circle a pond while cross-country skiing. These three types of pathways are often described as straight, zigzag, and curved. Together with the different directions, they can describe the spatial orientation of any movement you make.

Think of women in a basketball game. When would you see someone jump up and come down, facing forward the whole time? Can you think of a time when she might jump up facing forward and come down facing another direction? Consider the player dribbling the ball down the court while an opponent is trying to get the ball away from her. What would her pathway look like? She might move in several directions to avoid having the ball stolen.

The ball also makes different kinds of pathways, depending on the type of throw or pass that is used. Increasing your awareness of the spatial possibilities of an activity can be helpful in improving your skill, especially in team games. Being able to see a space created when a teammate moves to one side and then knowing how to use that space is an important skill to develop.

WHO OR WHAT YOU MOVE WITH

The basketball game provides an illustration of the third component of movement – relationships. Throwing, catching, kicking, hitting, dribbling, and rolling a ball are all examples of how you relate to an object by manipulating it. This relationship becomes even more complex when you use a racket, bat, or other implement. In addition, women might use javelins, paddles, shuttlecocks, hockey sticks, cue sticks, horseshoes, ribbons, and clubs as part of their movement activities.

Think about goal posts or hurdles. Even though women do not manipulate them, they are a vital part of certain activities. Women go over, under, around, through, on, into, out of, between, in front of, beside, or behind these and other objects such as gates, fences, diving boards, uneven parallel bars, trampolines, high-jump bars, and swimming pools.

The traditional activity-oriented view of movement restricts the use of objects; objects are rarely used in more than one way. The next time you have a chance, try some different ways of using equipment. Play tennis with a lacrosse stick instead of a racket. Use a swimming pool for running. Try a round ball that is weighted off center for a volleyball game.

One other category of relationships we haven't mentioned yet is relationships between and among people. Some activities, such as walking and archery, don't involve any movement relationships with other people. Sometimes you may be moving alone while surrounded by others who are also moving alone, as in swimming laps or doing calisthenics. In other activities you must work with or against others. Women can choose from a variety of activities where the movements of others are part of the game. Naturally, if an activity involves movement relationships with both objects and people, its spatial components are especially complex.

When only two people are involved, they may relate face to face, as in table tennis; in a leading-following relationship, as in canoeing; or side by side, as in running a race or in racquetball. Activities that involve more people have other possibilities for relationships: people forming circles, double circles, and lines as in dancing and synchronized swimming; a group of people surrounding one person as in softball; two groups or pairs of people facing each other as in badminton or volleyball; or two groups intermingling as in lacrosse, basketball, and soccer. Often, when two groups of people oppose each other many subdivisions and patterns can be identified within the overall movement pattern.

How You Move

Sometimes, how a motion is performed gives the movement a distinctive quality. Think of the difference between picking up a dime and picking up a piece of broken glass, or the difference between a drop shot and a smash in badminton. The motions could be identical, but the effort used for each is different.

To pick up a dime or smash the shuttlecock, you would use a firm or heavy touch. Picking up the broken glass would be safer with a fine or light touch, and a drop shot is effective because of the surprising lack of force. The motions are very similar, but the effort with which you move is different.

The speed of your movement can vary greatly depending on the effect you want. The most obvious difference between running and jogging is speed. Think of the different speeds you use when scrambling eggs and when adding dry ingredients to a bowl of cookie dough. Speed is an important factor in most movement activities. In manipulative activities, a slower speed is often used as a means of gaining control, as in putting in golf. A faster speed is often used to gain power, as in driving in golf.

The flow of movement is described by the words *sustained* (gradual) or *sudden* (jerky). Sudden movements are hammering a nail or using an ax. Sustained movements are coiling a rope or reeling in a fishing line. Both throwing an object and striking it (as in serving a tennis ball) usually have a fast speed, but striking has a more sudden impact on the object.

The flow of movement can often make an activity more or less appealing. Unless a person is exceptionally smooth in her motions, running is a series of fairly jerky movements, while cycling is mostly sustained movement. Similarly, calisthenics and jumping rope are mostly sudden, while yoga exercises and roller skating are smooth.

The final aspect of how you move is the direct or flexible use of space. Foil fencing is a very direct, linear activity, with only small deflections to the sides to parry a thrust or to clear the way for your own. On the other hand, fencing with a saber involves curving, slashing movements that fill up more of the space between you and your opponent.

Examining an activity to determine what parts of your body you move, your spatial awareness, your relationships to people and/or objects, and how you move can help you understand the kinds of movements and activities you enjoy most. By using these components to describe what you like and don't like, you can make changes to increase your enjoyment.

By knowing clearly what you prefer, you are also in a better position to choose and create new movement activities.

How you use the movement components determines your movement style. The more components you include in an activity, the more complex your style. Running in a straight line reflects a preference for a simple movement style. Running up and down hills or over obstacles as in cross-country running or hurdling adds complexity. Running in relationship to ten teammates, eleven opponents, a ball, and two goals is even more complex.

As more spatial awareness components are added, as in combining different directions and pathways, movements become increasingly complex. The most complex movements and activities involve multiple relationships among people, rules, and objects. A lacrosse game with twenty-four stick-carrying players all moving at once on a field that has two goals and markings on the ground is a highly complex situation. A person who enjoys throwing, catching, and cradling a ball with a crosse while positioning herself in relation to teammates, goals, and opponents has a complex movement style.

Use the skills and equipment you have. Imagine you are in a group of eight women and you have the usual equipment for a game of volleyball – net, ball, and flat playing area. You all want to play a game, but you don't really want to play volleyball. How can you go about making up a game to play?

One way to begin is to determine what you can do with the ball, how you can manipulate it, and what each woman especially enjoys doing with the ball. Then try to incorporate those elements into a game. If you choose to use the net, consider how you will use it. Determine the relationship the players will have to the ball. Will the ball go over or under the net? Will all eight women work together, or will groups of women work together against other groups?

Try your game. Modify it to take into account any special situations that arise. Make it as simple or complex as the group desires. Add rules or conditions that you need to make the game flow more smoothly or to provide breaks.

USING YOUR UNIQUENESS

Your movement style is unique. The movement activities you have chosen to participate in were formed by many factors, especially those in early childhood. Now is the time to develop a greater awareness of yourself as a mover and to actively seek movement forms that give you pleasure. Being aware of and creating your own movement style is part of the process.

How can you take what you know about your style, environment, movement components, and past activities and turn that knowledge into a working plan that will improve the quality of all your movement experiences? Following the lead of children is one possibility. When children play, they don't analyze and classify. They just do things they enjoy. When asked, they may describe or name their activity, but if not asked they probably wouldn't classify it. They don't put things in categories. The first part of your plan could be just to play — participate in activities simply for the fun of it. Initiate a game of throw and catch in the pool. Join an impromptu dance.

Children often change rules to suit the needs of the group. If the playing area is too small for kickball, they might shorten base paths and use a less bouncy ball. One of the most striking things about children's play is the way they make allowances for less skillful group members. Sometimes they create special roles so all their friends can be part of the game. Until they've absorbed the competitive sport ethic, children often don't see anything wrong with letting younger or less skilled players have some advantages to make up for their lack of experience or skill. Adults' games often are hooked on enforcing unbending rules that eliminate players who aren't "good enough" or that make playing unpleasant for less skilled players, but children's games usually focus on playing the game. Women can change this by being willing to modify or discard rules that eliminate players or detract from enjoyment.

Two special attributes of children's games that women could also imitate are organization and leadership. Children rarely have such large teams that they need uniforms to tell who's who. They don't depend on managers, umpires, and referees to enforce their rules. Through continued playing, they all know the rules well. They also know the consequences of breaking rules. If disagreements arise, the children involved may argue it out, with pressure from the rest of the group to settle the matter quickly so the game can continue. A common result of disagreement is repeating the play – starting over at some neutral point. This kind of enforcement of rules requires much more integrity and give-and-take among the players than does giving a nonplayer the power to run the game.

Women whose needs are met in formal league sports have the potential to change the coach's leadership behavior. The typical model is one in which a single person dictates what happens at practices and who plays what positions during games. Any input from team members into coaching decisions is through informal, indirect channels that are not accessible to all players. Women playing together on a team often have many skills and abilities that could be used to help the team as a whole. Certainly everyone has feelings and ideas about who should play what positions and when and how practices can be conducted. Even if a team wants to keep one person as the ultimate authority, there are ways to give each player access to the decision-making process rather than limiting access to only a few. Open discussions can give everyone a chance to have her say. Seeking out the expertise of team members can enrich the organization and improve skills during practice sessions. Team members can be allowed to make suggestions for starting line-ups. During games individuals can be encouraged to determine if they need to leave the game. Shared decision making makes team leadership more effective.

If the movement activities available to you do not seem to meet your needs, try to create your own options. If you want to be involved in an activity that requires special facilities without the formal trappings of clubs, classes, leagues, or referees, insist on a fair share of time for using those facilities. Don't be afraid to attempt changes in the traditional movement forms. Anything that enables you to experience your uniqueness while moving is worth trying.

BE A ROLE MODEL FOR CHILDREN

If you work with children or have your own children, you are probably concerned about their movement patterns and preferences. To encourage them to grow up to be comfortable and happy with movement, you can help them as well as yourself. Be active, both in activities that bring you pleasure and activities you engage in with children. Be the active, positive female role model you had or wish you'd had. As you experience or explore any of your own feelings of awkwardness, be sensitive to those of youngsters. Do not insist on perfection, especially in the early stages of learning new skills.

Encourage children to engage in a variety of activities and movement components. Help create a movement environment that encourages exploration and experimentation. Praise novel ideas and attempts at new skills. If you play with children, help them practice new skills by using one or two components, gradually adding more, so movement tasks won't be too complex at first. Don't ask a child to practice throwing for speed at the same time you ask for accuracy, for example.

When throwing to a child, use balls that are easy to grab and don't hurt. Toss them underhand from a distance that ensures your accuracy. At first, the child should only have to close her hands or arms around the ball—you must toss it to the right place! The same applies to batting and other striking skills.

There are a number of pieces of manipulative equipment you can make fairly inexpensively and use to encourage a variety of movements.

Hoops. Make hoops from one-half-inch flexible plastic tubing, available from a hardware store. Eight-foot lengths make good-sized hoops, but you can vary the length to make the hoops larger or smaller. Buy a plastic connector and place both ends of the tubing in very hot water for a minute or so before inserting the connector. That will help it go in farther and hold the hoop together better. Covering the connection with heavy-duty tape such as duct tape will make the connection hold for a long time.

Use hoops to twirl on the torso or body parts; for spinning or rolling; and for jumping over, into, or out of. Children can run through them while they are still or rolling. Hoops are an especially good tool for reinforcing spatial concepts.

Rings or smaller hoops. Use discarded garden hose, in any length that will keep its shape when the ends are connected. Put a three-inch-long dowel into each end, place the ends together, and wrap the whole area with overlapping layers of duct tape.

Rings may be used for the same activities as hoops. They are also good for throwing and catching, either in a vertical or horizontal position. It may be too hard for younger children to catch them in the air, but they might have fun catching them while they are rolling.

Jump ropes. Cotton rope about three-quarters of an inch in diameter is a good size and weight for a jump rope. Make two for each child so the children can use them to make tin-can stilts too. One way to measure the correct rope length is to have the child stand on the rope and hold an end in each hand at shoulder height with her elbows bent. Wrap duct tape tightly at both ends to prevent fraying. Besides using them for jumping, ropes can be placed on the floor or ground for walking on or beside, jumping over, and making pathways that are straight, curved, and zigzag.

Tin-can stilts. Two jump ropes and two cans are needed. Old gallon paint cans or 106-ounce cans from a cafeteria or supermarket are both good sizes; make sure they are well cleaned. Turn the cans upside down and use a punch-type can opener to punch two holes opposite each other right next to the rim. The holes should be big enough for the jump rope to go through easily, or you can use strong twine, nylon, or plastic cord. Tie the two ends of the rope together so when the child stands on the can the top of the rope is between hip and waist height.

To walk on the stilts, the child must use the rope to pull the can up and keep it in place as she moves one foot forward at a time. The stilts provide a novel form of balance and locomotion and can be used to travel in any direction or pathway. Some children may want to challenge themselves by walking up and down stairs or inclines or stepping over low obstacles.

Rackets. Homemade rackets are ideal for young children because they are lightweight and easily gripped by small hands. If bent out of shape, they may be easily bent back into shape. Take a coat hanger and pull the triangular part into a rounded paddle shape. Elongate and flatten the curved hanging part of the hanger.

One leg of nylon hosiery should be pulled over the hanger as far as possible, starting with the rounded surface and wrapping the excess nylon around the handle for padding. Secure the nylon to the handle with masking, adhesive, or duct tape. Use less hosiery for a smaller grip, and more tape or added nylon for a larger one. Wrap the tape around as many times as necessary to secure the nylon and to cover completely the open end of the hanger. If the toe of the hosiery does not fit tightly against the racket, make a "topknot" that pulls the nylon tight, secure it with tape, and cut off any excess nylon.

Nylon rackets may be held with one hand or two and used to swing at balloons, newspaper balls held together with tape, or lightweight foam balls such as Nerf balls. Children can practice hitting these objects on their own, or someone can pitch to them. The pitcher should first aim easy pitches where the child swings. When the child can adjust her own aim to hit objects in different places, throw them over her head and out to either side, eventually making her move in order to hit them. Gradually increase the speed of the throw.

As a woman in motion, you are a role model for girls and other women regardless of whether you wish to be. Your heightened awareness of movement environments, styles, and components not only helps create the meaningful movement experiences you deserve, but it also helps ensure wider options for other women and girls.

3
How to Begin Moving

ARE YOU AFRAID of developing "unsightly" muscles or are not sure you should be active during your menstrual period? Have you resigned yourself to a sedentary lifestyle because you believe your high percentage of body fat makes physical activity out of the question? Many women have such concerns and questions about their unique physiology and the effects of exercise. Most of their concerns, however, are based on fears or misconceptions that can easily be dispelled.

Realistically assess yourself. Stand in front of a mirror and take stock of your physical appearance. Decide if you're satisfied with what you see, or if you want to change something or make some improvements. Think of the clothes you wear: Do you find them attractive or do you wear what's necessary to mask certain parts of your physique? Take a look at your daily activities to see if you have sufficient energy to do all that is required of you and still have enough left over for leisure-time activities. When you're active, determine whether you like the way your body feels.

By asking how you feel about yourself, you can determine what your needs are and set appropriate goals to meet them. Gear yourself for success. If you don't match your goals to your needs, your movement activity may not lead to satisfaction or the perpetuation of movement.

MUSCLE AND FAT

Until recently, it was thought that muscle bulk was related to the hormone testosterone, which is normally found in much higher levels in men than in women. There is now uncertainty about this. Exercise physiologists are no longer sure that this hormone is responsible for muscle bulk, although no definitive alternative theory has been offered. The fact still remains that, for whatever reason, women's bodies do not produce as much muscle bulk as men's bodies.

Women who engage in activities that require a lot of strength and explosive power, like world-class shot putting and discus throwing, often take supplements that allow their bodies to produce the bulk they need. Many women do not want to emulate such female athletes. But even if you train as hard as they do, you will not necessarily look like them. Many women train very hard but never obtain that bulk. Some women are simply able to produce more bulk than others; it's an individual matter.

Fat and cellulite are other concerns of women. Cellulite is body fat that women usually associate with the ripples or dimply marks on their legs. These fat deposits cannot be eliminated through whirlpools, saunas, and steam baths. The only way you can get rid of body fat is through exercise and diet. When you decrease your percentage of body fat, you decrease the amount of cellulite. There's no other way. Dieting and shedding inches is just half the answer to the cellulite problem. The other half is exercise, since firm, taut muscles make you look slimmer.

In the process of eliminating fat through exercise, you may actually increase the size and weight of your legs or arms because you have also built up muscle, and muscle is heavier and denser than fat. By firming up, you may gain a little weight and inches, but the shape of your body will be different and it will be less flabby. The weight and inches you've gained are the fat you've turned into muscle. Maybe the little tightness you feel now in your clothes is from a nice, tight-looking leg or arm. Before, it was flabby, like a pillow stuck in your clothes. Now you've got something that has a firm shape.

It is true that women have more fat than men, and the reason is very simple: Women have breasts and bear children. Part of women's body fat is due to their breasts, which are mostly fatty tissue. Because of this, serious injuries to the breast from contact sports are very rare; breasts are not as vulnerable as some people lead you to believe. Women's pelvic areas also tend to be fattier than men's. This provides protection to the reproductive area in the event of a pregnancy.

These two factors do not mean that women are fatter than men and have to battle fat all their lives. Nor do they mean that because women have more body fat they cannot engage in certain activities. Once you understand that your extra fat consists of your breasts and the area around your reproductive system, you can realize that this is anatomically the way you are, and it does not prevent you from being active.

Many discussions and debates among athletes and physicians center on the usefulness of body fat. Some people say excess fat may be a burden for women who run long distances. Others think it is a burden in short distances because excess fat prevents women from having the necessary strength and explosive power. On the positive side, some say that excess body fat enables women to withstand temperature changes better than men. Because women have more fatty tissue, they have more energy stores in those tissues. Women therefore have the ability to go longer distances than men because they have more body fuel to rely on.

MENSTRUATION AND PREGNANCY

Women who engage in vigorous, intense, and regular exercise may find that either their periods stop or they bleed very little, and they aren't sure what this means. There has been no proof of a direct cause-and-effect relationship between exercise and lessened menstrual bleeding.

When an athlete starts intensive training or an inactive woman starts to exercise, her lifestyle, diet, and body composition will probably change. More physical stresses are put on the body as she exercises. An athlete who competes may add psychological stresses that can affect her hormone balance. Because the move to a more active lifestyle brings about these kinds of changes in a woman's life, it can't be said that exercise is the only factor if such a woman experiences lessened menstrual flow. Recent findings show that some women whose periods stop or whose flow lessens after beginning an exercise program have light or nonexistent periods to begin with. Menstrual irregularities were already apparent. Perhaps all the changes – in diet, lifestyle, and body composition – make such irregularities more pronounced. There is nothing to show that exercise brings them on.

Every woman's body reacts individually to a new exercise regimen. Exercise relieves menstrual discomfort for some women. For others, menstrual pain and discomfort are so acute they can't even think about exercising. Before menstruation, when a woman's hormones are changing and her body retains more fluid, she may find exercise, especially at a high level of intensity, more uncomfortable. But once her body has adapted or acclimated to these hormonal changes, she should have no problem engaging in exercise before her period.

Women sometimes feel guilty when they find exercise is satisfying during their period or a pregnancy. Women often handicap themselves with complaints about their periods – "I shouldn't do this today. I have my period" – but many such complaints are simply acculturated. Rarely do they have a physiological basis. Your mother said it. Your friends say it. You feel that if you don't complain about your period and if it doesn't somehow restrict or limit you, you're not part of the group. It's very hard when someone says, "I'm flowing so heavily and I have such bad cramps" to reply, "Wow! I could swim fifty laps or play three hours of tennis" when you're at the same stage of your cycle.

During pregnancy—especially in the early stages and toward the end—there may be times when a woman decreases her activity for a variety of reasons. Pregnant women can still work on stretching and keeping their muscles flexible and not allowing them to tighten or cramp. Rather than engaging in intense workouts, they can do a lot of stretching. But even in pregnancy the level of activity is an individual matter.

BY-PASSING SEX DIFFERENCES

Women tend to be smaller and have wider pelvises than men, which means they have a different running style. Women don't produce as much muscle bulk as men. But these differences are not important to physical activity. What women do with what they have—through conditioning or exercise—is the important thing: quality, not quantity. It doesn't matter how big you are or how lean, how long your arms are or how big your feet are. Women are able to do just about anything they want to do, regardless of anatomical or physiological differences.

Women tend to be much more flexible than men. But that doesn't stop men from being gymnasts or dancers. It is said that women are not as strong as men. But when women compete against each other in weightlifting or other activities involving strength, they're doing just as much as men. They're working at comparable levels.

Physiological differences are not limiting as long as you condition your body in the area in which you want to move. Through conditioning, you increase the muscle's energy capacity, thereby increasing the efficiency of your heart and circulatory system and reducing excess body fat. You can also increase your lung capacity and your ability to take in and use oxygen more efficiently. A man twice your size, maybe even twice as strong, may not be able to function at the same level as you because he may function less efficiently than you.

The amount of blood pumped by your heart with each beat is your stroke volume. The absolute stroke volume for women is smaller than it is for men. This is due to women's smaller size and their smaller hearts. During exercise, your heart can compensate for a lower stroke volume by beating more rapidly to sustain a sufficient amount of blood. As you become fit, your stroke volume will increase and your heart rate will decrease so that it can accomplish sufficient blood flow in fewer strokes.

When you increase your stroke volume, you increase the amount of blood that your heart can pump out. Your conditioning has also increased the amount of oxygen you can take in. Those two factors combine to increase the amount of oxygen that can be sent to your muscle cells. What is important is not just your capacity, but how much of your capacity you actually use – how efficiently your muscles are able to use the oxygen supply.

The idea that women are injured more frequently than men may have been true at one time, because women have not always been as well-conditioned or as fit as men. They have not had access to the same extensive conditioning, weight-training, or strength-training programs. Women do not get injured more than men, however, unless they set out to do something in a way that's likely to lead to injury, such as failing to stretch or warm up properly for an activity, using poor equipment, wearing inappropriate attire, or following faulty training methods. And under such conditions, men are just as prone to injury as women. Injuries are more activity-related than gender-related.

Osteoporosis – or the loss of bone mass – is increasingly becoming recognized as a serious problem among older women. A woman who has reached menopause or who has had a total hysterectomy no longer produces estrogen. Estrogen deficiencies cause menopausal women to lose about 1 percent of their bone mass per year. This is why women are more prone in later years to spontaneous and nonspontaneous bone breaks. Men lose proportionally less bone mass per year, so they are not prone to breaks until their eighth decade. Women can take estrogen orally and can also exercise to help reduce osteoporosis. Without physical activity, bone atrophy occurs. Active women therefore tend to lose less bone mass than do sedentary women.

EXERCISING

In the past decade, aerobic exercise and dance have attracted a following. The term *aerobic* (in the presence of oxygen) refers to the body's process of transporting oxygenated blood to the muscles. The fuel required for contraction of muscle cells is provided by the blood transport system from the chemical storage of digested foods and, if that is insufficient, from the breakdown of the body's tissues. To burn the fuel, the muscle cells draw on their own chemistry for a relatively short period of time (anaerobic metabolism, or metabolism in the absence of oxygen), after which they require the assistance of oxygen (aerobic metabolism).

Every exercise involves an anaerobic phase while the blood transport system is mobilizing and adapting to the greater demand of muscular work. One key purpose of a warmup period is to give this mobilization a head start. If muscle demands are met by circulating oxygen and fuel, a steady state is achieved and the onset of fatigue is postponed, meaning the body can engage in effective exercise for a sustained period. Aerobic exercise refers to a prolonged, steady state of exercise as opposed to short-term exercises that do not put demands on the aerobic energy pathway.

Your blood functions as a transportation system, bringing fuel in the form of oxygen to your organs, which include your muscles, and then removing the carbon dioxide and lactic acid as waste products. There is always blood in your muscles, but when your heart works more efficiently you extract more oxygen from the blood and put it into the tissues so you can run your body longer and harder.

Developing endurance, the ability to repeatedly perform work against a light load for an extended period, requires increased efficiency of the blood supply system. First, women who become involved in endurance training must decide on frequency of training – three times a week is necessary if you want to improve, twice a week is enough to maintain fitness; second, duration of workouts – twenty minutes is minimum; and third, intensity, which will change as your level of fitness increases.

The simplest and most practical way to determine your own level of intensity – the amount of exercise you have to do to challenge your system effectively – is to take your pulse. Your exercise pulse rate, the one at which you should be exercising for endurance, can be figured as roughly 60 to 75 percent of your maximum heart rate, or 220 minus your age. This number will give you a pulse rate that you can gradually work up to. You should be able to sustain the rate for twenty to thirty minutes of exercise.

There are more exact ways to accurately determine your exercise work load, such as an exercise stress test, which gives a precise maximum heart rate you can attain . You can calculate the amount of carbon dioxide you expire compared to the oxygen you take in to determine the intensity at which you should exercise. Your skin temperature also can give some clues about the efficiency of your system. Unless you have a particular problem or cardiac risk factors, however, a rough estimate based on your pulse rate is sufficient to determine an appropriate level of exercise.

Your movement activities should include flexibility exercises, which are useful in performing specific skills as well as in your overall health and fitness. In addition, an increase in flexibility can decrease the severity and occurrence of some injuries. The best exercises to use for flexibility are the so-called stretching exercises. These can be performed either by holding a stretched position for a given amount of time or by using bouncing and bobbing movements without holding the final stretched position. While both types of stretching improve flexibility, the static method is preferred because it requires less energy, relieves muscular soreness, and avoids the risk of tearing muscle fibers that comes with bouncing.

Stretching is also an excellent way to warm up and cool down. Warming up is used to help prevent injury, increase the blood flow to muscles, and make muscles more responsive and alert. Some women find it beneficial to move around (walking or jogging) until they feel warm and loose, and then engage in stretching. This method is not as painful as stretching a cold muscle. Cooling down after vigorous exercise may take a few minutes longer than warming up and should be an extremely gradual process that allows the bodily functions to slowly return to a pre-exercise state. Flexibility and/or stretching exercises should be a part of every exercise session.

STRENGTH TRAINING

Many women have begun training to develop strength, which is the force exerted by a muscle or muscle group against a resistance. Weight machines and free weights are used in a strength-training program. Free weights are supported by the weightlifter herself and do not have any attachments, as are barbells and dumbbells. Weight machines offer different stations that work on specific muscle groups. Machines differ in the range of resistance offered.

The following questions and answers are useful to anyone organizing a strength-training program for proper use of the weights.

- What exercises should be performed?

    The exercises will depend on the equipment available. The total body should be worked, which means at least one exercise for each of the major muscle groups. Performing the exercises correctly and with regularity is usually more important than which exercises are performed.

- How much weight should be used in each exercise, and with how many repetitions?

A person using weight machines should perform between eight and twelve repetitions of each exercise for the upper body. The same number is to be used for the lower body. A weight should be selected, through trial and error, that will cause the person to reach the point of muscular failure within these limits. Muscular failure has been reached when the person can no longer raise the weight in good form through the muscle's full range of motion.

All-out attempts to determine how much weight you can lift will lead to injury and are not as effective as performing more repetitions with less weight. It is not *how much* weight you lift that produces results, but *how* you lift the weight. A properly performed exercise includes a full range of motion in which the muscles are responsible for raising and lowering the weights. Proper supervision is also important if the weight-training program is to be safe and beneficial.

The overload principle must be observed if a woman is to increase her level of strength. This principle states that for improvement to occur, a greater than normal demand must be placed on the muscular system. An individual should not sacrifice form or technique to increase the demand, however.

- In what order should exercises be performed?

Whenever possible, women should exercise the larger and stronger muscles of the body first. Progress from the muscles of the legs to the torso, to the arms, and finish with the muscles of the abdomen. Although no specific order is superior to all others, you should group your exercises by body parts and alternate pushing and pulling movements for the torso and arm muscles.

• How much rest should be taken between exercises?

For those who have the time and inclination, resting between exercises is a good idea, but it prolongs the training session. Moving nonstop from one exercise to the next takes less time and places greater demand on the cardiovascular system, thereby increasing an individual's overall level of fitness. Those who participate in both strength exercises and aerobic or endurance activities (jogging, swimming, aerobic dance), have little reason to use the strength exercises to place greater demands on the cardiovascular system.

• How many sets of each exercise should be performed?

When lifting weights, repetitions of an exercise are grouped into sets. One properly performed set on weight machines is recommended to stimulate optimal gains in muscular strength and endurance. If a woman properly performs one set, she will certainly not feel able to perform a second set. If she can perform a second set at a high level of intensity, she has not done the first set properly.

More than one set can be done using free weights because a person can be injured by performing one set until she cannot lift the weight or can no longer perform the exercise correctly. When using free weights, even if done in proper form, a woman should be sure a spotter is always present to guard against the danger of injury.

• How many workouts should be undertaken per week?

If you want to maintain your condition, you need to work out twice a week. If you want to improve, you need at least three sessions a week. Many people working out at clubs or gyms have been told to rest for a day between training sessions. In general, this is a good idea if you work your muscles to the point of muscular failure. An overloaded muscle needs forty-eight to seventy-two hours to fully recover. Most people don't fatigue their muscles sufficiently to need this rest period. Some people like to tone their muscles daily, and they may choose a heavy exercise session one day and a light one the next.

STARTING OUT

There are many activities that can be done without formal instruction. Walking and bicycling are especially appropriate because of their self-pacing nature: You can challenge yourself as much or as little as you like. Other possibilities can be determined by your interests, past activities, and willingness to experiment. You may be able to revive your skills in an activity you used to enjoy.

When starting something new, you should be particularly concerned about safety and injury prevention, and it is a good idea to have a physical examination before entering a new activity. Safety considerations are usually based on common sense and forethought, which women who are accustomed to caring for themselves or others usually have in abundance. Each woman must learn to listen to her body and feelings to prevent personal injury. She must learn to recognize her own symptoms of overexertion and strain. The process of learning to play tennis after five or ten years of relative inactivity, for instance, should be a slow and easy one; it should allow for breaks, if necessary, before the completion of a game or set.

One way to make the transition to risk-taking activities is to look for ways to vary your own routine and usual activities. Try this: Think of a situation in which you are just a little bit uncomfortable — playing golf with someone who is better than you or joining a volleyball or softball team, for example. The next time the situation presents itself, seize it as an opportunity to do what you are afraid of. Do whatever you need to do to nudge yourself into action. Afterward, notice how you feel. If you feel good in some way, try it again in the same situation or a different one. Try to stretch out and hold on to that good feeling by thinking or talking about it. It's all right to ask for help from anyone at any time.

Once you've committed yourself to a new activity, you may need small challenges to keep yourself going. In the middle of a long run, promise yourself a short time of walking if you can continue running to the next driveway or mailbox. If your goal is to run two miles, it might be important to work up to it gradually, getting comfortable with a quarter-mile run at first and then daring to double it. The encouragement of a friend or partner can be indispensable.

SETTING GOALS

One way for women to assure themselves of regular participation in movement activities is to set reasonable and obtainable goals. Women who haven't defined what they want run the risk of feeling gypped. Those who feel the satisfaction of achievement have won something by establishing and then reaching a specific goal. It is a wonderfully satisfying feeling to set a goal and to achieve it.

Most women are used to having goals set for them by parents, teachers, or spouses. They have been taught to believe that focusing on themselves will deprive others of their energies and hurt others by their selfishness. Concentrating on self-development is made difficult for most women because they have been so thoroughly instructed to bolster the needs of other people first.

As more and more women are realizing, it's perfectly all right to determine your own future and concentrate on doing what benefits you. It doesn't diminish what you do to help your husband, children, or parents. The affection and relationships you've always had will remain while you grow and develop in your own way. Setting personal goals and standards doesn't mean loss—it's a winning process all the way.

Give some time and attention to yourself. Be introspective and honest. Write down your goals and save them, referring to them as your needs and self-knowledge strengthen and change. The following are some possible goals that can affect your physical well-being:

- Social contacts
- Weight loss or control
- Approval of others
- Health concerns (heart, blood pressure)
- Rehabilitation
- Strength
- Status
- Flexibility
- Escape
- Fun

Goals are a very personal matter. Any motivating force is valid as long as you're completely honest with yourself. A goal casually set and lightly taken is freely abandoned at the first obstacle. What you establish in writing as your goals is your strength. There is power in it. It is your fuel, the force that will drive you.

How will you reach your goals? Certainly not in one giant leap. The way to do it is by setting short-term goals, productive objectives you can realistically attain. Darcy actively sets short-term and long-term goals. She commits them to paper so she can see where she has been, where she is now, and how far she has to go. It also helps her combat feelings of not getting anywhere that come when she is depressed, angry, or discouraged. By looking at her schedule of goals for the first month, six months, or perhaps the first year of exercise, she can see if she's moving along at a reasonable pace or if she needs to revise some of her goals.

It is important to have some measure of progress. Find some method of keeping track of body weight, pulse rate, blood pressure, distances run, weights lifted, or laps swum. Periodic and meaningful reexamination of goals is of great value. It measures progress toward stated goals and allows redefinition of them if that is appropriate. Darcy said, "Unless I have a clear plan, I'm apt to feel overwhelmed or feel I'll never get it all done, and then I'll do nothing. With a structure, though, I merely have to execute the plan step by step and it just seems to flow along."

STAYING ON COURSE

If you choose an activity that requires good weather and you live in a cold, snowy, and rainy climate, you've already built in a chance not to succeed. If there's an activity you really want to do, try to find a setting in which it can be done year-round. You can join a tennis club for year-round tennis or run on an indoor track in bad weather. It's a human weakness to set out to do something in such a way that one does not allow oneself the chance to succeed. Don't cut yourself off from success before you begin: Choose several activities that can be done in alternate seasons, or choose an activity that can be done year-round.

Some people like seasonal activities. Others don't like changes in activity. They need to do one activity with regularity, regardless of the season. Tune into yourself and recognize your strengths and choose an activity accordingly.

The activity you choose should be complementary to your job. If you have a sedentary job and you choose to do something like archery or golf, you may wonder why you don't feel better or see any results. You haven't complemented your routine or your lifestyle. The activity is similar to the type of job you have. You've done nothing to give yourself a break, a lift, or a change.

If your job requires a great deal of physical strength or exertion and you choose to engage in an activity that requires physical exertion, you may be constantly tired. You probably need to choose something a little more relaxing, some activity that doesn't involve so much explosive movement.

If you constantly deal with people in your job and you choose to go to a group exercise class or a crowded spa, you may wonder why you feel as if you have no time to yourself. You probably need a more individual or solitary type of activ-

ity. If you see very few people in your job, then you may want
to be involved in a group activity with a lot of verbal and
physical interaction. It may be advantageous for you to be in
a setting where you can make social contacts outside your
job.

Of course, some people are very happy with a sedentary job
and a movement form that requires very little physical exertion or with physically demanding jobs and activities. Each
person needs to determine for herself the kind of activity that
suits her personality or her place of residence, complements
her job and its requirements, and is suitable to do year-round.

Staying on course may also be easier if you have a partner.
The partner you select should be one who can understand
your needs and provide useful support. This person should be
someone whose judgment you respect and who respects
yours. You should define your goals together, discuss their
reality, and build into your relationship some regular contact
for reviewing your progress toward those goals. When you
stray from your purpose or are unconcerned about losing
 time, your partner can help steer you back on course through
feedback and constructive advice. You can do the same in
return. The buddy system is worth its weight in gold if working with or meeting with a partner helps you make and keep
commitments.

Finding a partner is not always easy. Sometimes the right
individuals just aren't available to you. If you are really on
your own, you can create a support system by getting help in
one area from one person, adding to it with help in another
area from a second person, and so on. The object is to have
wise and helpful people assist you in setting and reaching
specific goals.

WORKING OUT ON YOUR OWN

For women with a low budget or with no inclination to be
part of a group, there are alternatives to group activities. You
can dance to a record or follow stretching exercise sessions on

television. Buy a jump rope. If you want to make more of an investment, buy a stationary bicycle or a set of free weights for stretching and toning. You can work on cardiovascular endurance and toning up your legs while you're watching television or reading a book. Some bicycle models allow you to adjust the resistance to simulate riding uphill, and some also come with a clock and odometer. Whatever you decide to invest in, be sure to use it. Having your own equipment is not going to help you if you let it gather dust.

Whether you do it at home, at the office, or in your community, it is important when you're exercising on your own to make your activity part of your routine. Pick a convenient time of day. If you want to do it at work, locate an available space or room, a record player, some mats – whatever you need. Make sure this room is available to you at the same time every day and build it into your own schedule. Find a resource person. Write away for information. Be active in finding the right environment for solitary activity.

Do some exploring. Take some risks. You can stay active as long as you have confidence in yourself.

4
Health Clubs

REMAINING ACTIVE or making the transition from a sedentary lifestyle to an active lifestyle does not necessitate joining a health spa or club. A good club, however, can help a woman obtain both fitness and fun. Health clubs provide services and facilities to aid clients in the improvement of their physical condition through weight control and exercise.

Before deciding whether this is an appropriate option for you, become aware of your fears. Why would you hesitate to join a club? Once you joined, why might you stop going? What has scared you away from seeking out a membership in the past?

To overcome your fears, real or imagined, your major weapon is knowledge. By knowing as much as you can about a new situation you can greatly reduce and perhaps eliminate your fear of the unknown. It is also possible, through knowledge, to better prepare yourself for the changes in scheduling brought on by a new undertaking.

The fear of failure is very real, but the more you know about a new situation, the less likely you are to fail. Knowledge helps you become more realistic about your goals. You have a better understanding of what you can expect to get from a particular experience. Meeting with success and achieving goals bring with them the confidence you need to deal with criticisms and obstacles you might encounter.

Getting to the point of feeling confident is not always easy. Gale has experienced this. She was once a professional dancer, but she stopped dancing when she married and had two children. Maintaining a daily exercise routine remained a part of her life. Now that her children are in school, Gale has gone to work full time and is in a high-powered executive position. Gale feels she has no time for herself, least of all for exercise. She seldom enjoys a complete evening at home with her family because she always has meetings or brings work to do at home.

Recently, Gale noticed that she's losing her flexibility, her energy level has decreased drastically, and her once firm, taut muscles now sag. She is neither as loose nor as relaxed as she was when she was dancing. Gale refuses to take any more time away from her family but is tense and tired whenever she is with them.

Knowledge could have helped Gale. She needed to know that a little time spent away from her family doing exercises would have lessened her tension and improved her relations with her family in the long run. Just knowing she was not the only one who felt or looked run-down and out of shape would have helped, too. Contact with women similar to herself might have been a source of much-needed support.

Health clubs can fill this kind of need. They provide a social atmosphere in which being a woman and being active are not mutually exclusive. Women can work on strength, endurance, flexibility, and a suitable movement form, along with self-confidence. Racquetball courts, whirlpools, gyms, and other facilities offer many alternatives for the woman who is not sure what activity she wants or who knows she enjoys a variety of activities. The services and facilities can be vastly different from club to club, leaving prospective members the proper selection of the club that best meets their individual needs.

WHY JOIN?

It is important to be clear and honest with yourself about your goals and about how much time and money you are realistically willing to devote to achieve them. The only way to find out if a club is right for you is to visit it to see if it has the type of atmosphere you can comfortably work in.

Some women join clubs for the supervision and instruction. They want to be monitored, watched, corrected, instructed, and helped along to their goals. They do not feel they have the knowledge or motivation to do this on their own or with a friend at home. These women may not have exercised in a long time, may never have exercised properly, or may not have learned how to improve or intensify their present workout. Clubs with adequate personnel offer women the opportunity to constantly check whether they are doing exercises correctly. Women also become members of health clubs for access to the weight machines, saunas, swimming pools, steam rooms, and other facilities. They carry out a program they have already set for themselves. But most women join because they need the constant attention to motivate them to stay involved on a regular basis. Constant reevaluation and proof of how well they're doing moves them toward their goals.

Making a financial investment may be the key to taking yourself and a program seriously. Exercise at home may occur only sporadically, no matter how hard you try. If you've paid money for a program, however, you may feel more committed and obligated to put in some extra effort.

Perhaps you're concerned about being in socially acceptable surroundings. If so, your choice of a club and its setting may be crucial to your success. Your ability to adhere to a program will be enhanced if you feel comfortable in, and even proud of, the people and facilities around you. Once your confidence improves and you become self-motivated, you may find these considerations less important.

WHAT'S RIGHT FOR YOU?

A club's emphasis is important. Is it low-key and relaxed yet demanding, or is it run like a training ground for the Olympics? Can the whole family participate? Are day-care services provided? Is there more socializing than moving? Do the personnel give you the individual attention and counseling you require? Is there too much supervision? Will you leave the facility feeling relaxed or tense, tired or energetic, satisfied or dissatisfied?

Some other considerations when you look for an appropriate health club are the following:

- Is it conveniently located so you can drop in during your lunch hour or a break in your daily schedule?
- Is it on a bus route, within walking distance, or close to adequate parking?
- Will you be able to go through your activities in the time you can allot?
- Can you choose to engage in activities alone or with others?
- Is it for women only or for men and women?
- Will you need any special clothing or equipment?
- Does the atmosphere fit your personality?

The name of a club may be misleading. The title alone may not tell you what the personnel, equipment, and emphasis are. A fitness center in one city may be called a spa in another. Until you actually visit a club and see for yourself how it operates, you have no way of telling whether it will help you meet your goals.

A certain brand or equipment or company name is no guarantee of a club's quality. A club is only as good as its personnel and their knowledge about the facilities. There's no use paying for a lot of expensive equipment if you don't learn to use it properly. The reverse is true as well: The expertise of the staff can only go so far if you're unable to perform a workout because of a lack of apparatus. You want to have the best available combination of well-maintained equipment and experienced, knowledgeable personnel.

To satisfactorily meet your goals and to devise a successful program, consider this three-step process:

- Determine how physically fit you are.
- Identify how physically fit you want to be.
- Develop a program for overcoming the difference between what you are and what you want to be.

You can determine how physically fit you are by asking yourself two general questions: Do you look the way you want to look? Are you physically able to do what you need to do at work, home, or leisure? If your answer to both questions is yes, all you need is a program to maintain what you've got. If your answer to either question is no, then you need to look further for a program or environment that allows you to meet your specific goals.

Depending on your own situation, you may need a doctor's advice to determine how physically fit you reasonably want to be. A doctor can give you advice about how physically fit you can reasonably hope to be. This will make it easier to develop and participate in a program that can best achieve your personal goals. Commit yourself to a program that is both sensible and scientifically sound. Specific overall conditioning programs vary from individual to individual depending on personal goals and equipment available. Keep in mind that it is not possible to overcome months and years of self-neglect overnight.

Some clubs ask everyone over thirty-five to have clearance from a doctor. It is a good idea that anyone starting out on a new fitness regimen consult a doctor, especially if you are following this three-step process to develop an individualized program. If you've had a recent operation or infection or conditions such as hypertension and respiratory and heart problems, it is important to find out if your doctor recommends any limitations before you start your program. There are very few conditions that should keep you out of a health club.

You may want to reject a facility if you are not satisfied that you'll be able to receive ongoing professional attention.

This attention – commonly referred to as follow-up – helps hold each party accountable to the program. If the goals are set realistically, they should be attainable and allow you to see and feel results. If the counselor devises a sample program for you, have the counselor explain when and how the follow-ups will occur. Checking results periodically assures you that the program is suitable and your goals are being met.

A follow-up is not merely a checkup that takes place every few weeks. Quantitative measurements should take place periodically to reassess and reset your goals and your program. To have successful results at these checkpoints, it is necessary to have had some ongoing consultations and guidance. A counselor who is truly interested in you and not just your money will attend to you or at least check in with you each time you are present. He or she should check whether:

- you properly execute exercises and use weight machines;
- the prescribed amount of exercise or weight is adequate;
- the parts of the body not involved in a particular exercise are relaxed;
- you are breathing properly and rhythmically and exhaling as force is exerted;
- your dietary habits are appropriate; and
- you engage in activities that supplement or complement your regular program.

Above all, however, the way you feel is the best barometer of the program's suitability for you.

SALES TACTICS

The more expensive a club is, the better are your chances of being exposed to a hard sell. Figure salons do not usually need to employ high-pressure tactics to secure new members because their fee is nominal. The price of a membership can be as little as three or four dollars a month if you take advantage of a promotional ad or two-for-one discount.

Rarely is the price more than $10 a month. Although it is not possible to join many types of clubs for this price, it is possible to obtain a membership at some for a very reasonable rate. Remember, however, that the facilities of many figure salons are limited to exercise equipment. Showers, lockers, whirlpools, and competent guidance may be totally lacking.

Membership prices usually vary according to the time of year. Most people join clubs in spring and summer. As warmer weather and bathing suit season approach, most women begin to see themselves differently. A good time to visit a club is around the Christmas holiday season. The best price deals are available at the end of the year. Few people have the time, money, or inclination to join a club during the holiday season, and clubs need to lure potential members with discount offers and gift certificate reductions.

The most common choices of clubs other than figure salons are Nautilus centers, YMCAs and YWCAs (or other organizations beginning with "Y"), and spas. Nautilus centers are usually equipped with exercise machines that work on every area of the body. Some of these centers also have whirlpools, saunas, showers, and lockers. The staff is well educated and informed in proper use of the machines. The average cost of such a center is $200-$300 a year. Health spas are fully equipped with exercise machines and free weights along with sauna, whirlpool, steam room, and sun room. They may also include a track, pool, and racket courts. The staff is trained to sell and may not be as well trained in how to exercise properly. Such clubs charge between $200 and $700 a year. Y's are usually less expensive than health clubs. Their equipment may not always be in the best condition, but for women who cannot afford luxurious exercising, they are a good buy.

When you visit a club, you may come in contact with a counselor. This person may be one you specifically requested or is the counselor available for the next potential sale. If there's one thing a counselor learns in the mandatory monthly sales-training sessions, it is that sales are made on the tour, not in the office. From the moment you meet the counselor, she or he will ascertain as much medical and personal information about you as possible, under the guise of individualizing a program specifically for you. The counselor will use this information to categorize you and determine the appropriate script to make a sale.

An individualized program may consist of a twenty-to-thirty-minute workout, including strength and endurance activities on various pieces of equipment, flexibility floor exercises, and aerobic activities. A group exercise session may be included in the program. It's a good idea to wear or bring exercise clothing when you visit prospective clubs. The exercises and pieces of equipment are specially chosen, as are the introductions to certain members. Just as the counselor has a prepared script, so can you. Part of your script should be to test the equipment and the personnel.

The fact that a counselor follows a prepared sales pitch does not mean she or he is not well qualified in the area of fitness. If you are impressed by everything about the club except the knowledge of the counselor, don't automatically reject the club. Instead, find out if there is an employee who is qualified to advise you on a suitable program. It's possible, after all, that you have simply drawn an inexperienced counselor in a club that does have some well-trained personnel. An astute counselor who cannot answer some of your questions will quickly refer you to a colleague who can. You should then direct your prepared questions to that person. In this way, you will be able to evaluate the club based on the best personnel it has to offer. If your original counselor does not lead you to a competent source without some nudging, you must take the initiative. Remember, you are in the driver's seat. You have something the counselor wants – money. Make it clear that you are determined to be fully satisfied before money changes hands. When this becomes obvious to the counselor, the burden is on her or him to offer satisfaction. If it is not offered, chances are you won't be satisfied at that particular club.

To get a sense of the accuracy of the information being conveyed to you, you can ask questions that you know the answers to or you can call upon your common sense. Look for logical, clear, and direct answers to your questions. Don't accept vague terms. You might also test the counselor by asking questions about equipment that is not included in the tour. Frequently, poorly trained counselors know little about the club's facilities that are not on the tour. Other questions you might ask include the following:

- Why are exercises done in a specific position, a designated number of times, and with a prescribed amount of weight?
- What should I be doing on the days I don't go to the club?
- What are some exercises for those target areas that can be done at home?
- Is there any information on nutrition or diet?

During the exercise period, try to speak with members other than the ones who were introduced. Also, note the equipment's state of repair, how much it is being used, and if there is a full complement of machines for total body exercise.

Some clubs allow tours only at certain times, usually the times when the place is least crowded. That is to give you the impression that you will always have all the time you need and you will not have to wait for equipment or personnel when you work out.

While cooling down from your sample workout, you may be told that you will view the spa area and then go to the office to talk about the available membership plans. Spa areas may have any or all of the following: whirlpool, sauna, steam room, pool, sun room, and massage room. The visit to the spa area should include information on the safe and proper use of each area and its physiological benefits. Sometimes a counselor cites false benefits to be derived from spa facilities—that whirlpools will reduce body fat and rid you of unsightly cellulite, that the sauna will give you a flawless complexion, that the steam room will cure your sinus problems. Basically, the spa facilities increase the flow of blood, which in turn carries away the muscles' waste products produced from exercising. The warm temperature of the steam room is especially relaxing if you are tight and sore after exercise. The warm, moist air is also good for mild upper-respiratory congestion.

For the sauna to be beneficial, the temperature must be extremely high and the air very dry. The object of the sauna is to get your skin temperature higher than the temperature of the core of your body (usually it's the other way around). This increase in skin temperature increases circulation, bringing blood to the tiny vessels on the surface, which are usually not used. Small sweat glands open, cleansing pores in areas like the skin on your legs, where you ordinarily don't perspire. Saunas may be good for you by increasing the circulation of blood to the surface of the skin. Your complexion may improve somewhat as a result, but the sauna will not eliminate acne. If at any time you feel faint, dizzy, or have a rapid pulse, leave the sauna immediately.

Women at clubs frequently ask, "Can I burn calories by sitting in the whirlpool?" The answer is no. Through water agitation and heat, the whirlpool offers a combination of a massaging action and a hot-water bath. This combination increases circulation and produces a soothing sensation. The increase in circulation can cause faintness and dizziness. Therefore, the whirlpool is best used for short intervals (three to five minutes) in the beginning, until you find your tolerance level for heat.

Besides assuring yourself of the physiological benefits of the club's facilities, do another type of observing during the initial tour. One thing to note in both the gym and spa areas is the permanence of the installed equipment. Are the machines secured or can they be removed easily? Are the whirlpools and showers portable or built-in? Has the club invested in a swimming pool, track, or racquetball court? In other words, could the club easily move out overnight and take your money with it, or is it here to stay?

When you finally go to the office for the sell, one of two things can happen. If you go into the office knowing exactly what you want and what you are willing to pay for it, this can be an enjoyable and mutually beneficial experience. On the other hand, if you are unknowing and unsuspecting, you can walk out of the office confused and broke.

Different tactics and phrases are used to get you to sign on the spot. Some salespeople will appeal to your vanity, asking such questions as "Just how long have you been overweight? Does it run in your family?" or "Who else in your family has weight problems?" Other tactics are used to unsettle you, making you feel guilty or inadequate if you express any reluctance about joining: "Are you going to allow someone else to make this important decision for you? Can't you make up your own mind?" or "Wouldn't your spouse prefer to see you in better shape?"

Another method is for the counselor to ask only "yes" questions. If the counselor has given you an excellent exercise tour and has allowed you to use all the services and facilities, she or he knows that the answer to the following questions will be yes, hopefully including the last question as well: Did you enjoy the exercise tour and the use of the spa area? Could you feel how each piece of equipment works on a specific part of the body? Do you feel more relaxed, yet somehow more invigorated? Do you think we have the facilities and personnel necessary to help you achieve your goals? If we could come up with a membership that fits your needs and pocketbook, would you sign today? Good, let's get started!

For the counselor, the ideal way to get started would be with a long-term contract. If the long-term contract is what you want, and it is a significantly better deal financially, go for it. Otherwise, a short-term contract gives you the time necessary to determine if this club is going to meet all your needs. A trial period offers a chance to realistically assess your degree of commitment, enabling you to determine if a long-term contract is worth the price.

Certain discounts are usually available to the consumer. If you are accompanied by a member of the club, or if you enroll with another person, such as your spouse or a friend, you may be quoted discount prices. Some clubs offer a free option to short-term members of an automatic conversion to a life-time membership upon their recruitment of two other members within a specified period of time. Another way to receive a discount is to take advantage of promotional ads.

Unfortunately, a lot of people start out enthusiastically and then, when the novelty wears off, use the club rarely if at all. This phenomenon is one that clubs count on: They often sell more memberships than they can handle on the expectation that some members won't use the facilities regularly. Bear this in mind as you look for a facility to suit your needs. Look for all the requirements necessary to enable you to stick with it comfortably, conveniently, and enjoyably. Then you will be willing to pay for it and it will be worth the cost because you will make use of it.

Remember that, in all likelihood, the person who is trying to sell you a membership will literally be profiting from a sale. The counselor turned salesperson will get your attention by using your name and finding out everything possible about you. This person's sales experience will be used to subtly mirror your desires, adding to this how the benefits cannot be obtained on your own or without the club's services and personnel. Closing on a contract is a skill the salesperson has probably practiced for some time. She or he can wait until you make the "right" decision.

Though not a typical story, the following incident actually happened in the sales office of a health club. One day when the club's owner was making his weekly visit, a woman fainted in the office during the sales pitch. The woman, in her twenties, had worked at a sedentary office job and had never had exercise as an integral part of her daily life. She had hypertension and great anxieties about this first encounter at an exercise facility.

The counselor who took her on the tour allowed this woman to try only the exercises and machines. A normal tour of twenty to thirty minutes was cut to ten minutes because of her history. All the excitement, however, caused her to pass out in the middle of the counselor's sales pitch.

The counselor called to the owner for help. While he was reviving the woman, he and the counselor said such things as "It should be absolutely clear to you now how badly you are in need of an exercise program. You are only in your twenties with a husband and two children who depend on you, and you can't make it through ten minutes of mild exercise. How will you make it through life? There should be no reason for anyone here to have to *try* to sell you a membership after this incident. It would be obvious to anyone in your position that an immediate physical conditioning program is in order, especially if you want to enjoy a certain quality of life with your family." She signed up for a lifetime membership on the spot.

Despite the abuses in this relatively young industry, there are significant benefits to joining a club. Chief among these — especially for those who are not self-starters — are the convenience and regularity these exercise programs offer.

COMPARING OPTIONS

For some women, becoming aware of local exercise facilities is quite novel. Available facilities as well as their names vary from locale to locale. Besides Y's, Nautilus centers, figure salons, and spas, other options are adult education classes at colleges or high schools, parks and recreation department programs, country clubs, racket clubs, and dance studios.

YMCAs and YWCAs usually offer a wide variety of activities in a low-key atmosphere that emphasizes recreation and a philosophy of play. Offerings include dance classes, team and individual sports, self-defense, yoga, swimming, weight training, calisthenics, gymnastics, and slimnastics. These range in level from beginner to advanced. Most Y's have fairly well equipped exercise rooms (free weights, Nautilus or Universal machines), with enough equipment to exercise all the parts of the body.

Classes are open to all; nonmembers pay a higher fee than members. Membership prices vary with location and extent of facilities, but generally they are reasonably priced. Babysitting or day-care services may be available. Y's sometimes have spa areas as well. These facilities, except showers and lockers, are usually reserved for individuals who hold certain types of memberships.

Parks and recreation departments have the same philosophy as Y's, and some have as many varied class offerings and levels. Classes are not always held in a central location as at Y's. Parks and recreation departments use facilities and personnel that are available in the surrounding community. Normally there is only a nominal fee for these classes.

Adult education classes stress education through participation, rather than a sport emphasis. Classes might include physical fitness, aerobic dancing, ballroom dancing, backpacking and hiking, yoga, racket sports, and swimming. Offerings differ widely according to available personnel and facilities and are reasonably priced.

Fitness centers can be coed or restricted to one sex. More and more women-only clubs are opening. The facilities can range from sheer luxury to stark simplicity. They may be luxurious enough to include plush carpeting and furniture, extensive weight-training equipment, tracks, tennis or racquetball courts, pools, sun rooms, saunas, whirlpools, massage rooms, juice bars, daily class offerings, day-care services, and very valuable one-to-one instruction and counseling. Or the entire facility may be housed in one large room with one or two employees, several exercise classes, adequate equipment, and no showers or lockers. In between is every combination imaginable. Obviously, the more a club offers, the higher its price. Look carefully because what best suits your budget may not suit your needs.

Dance studios offer a multitude of classes for all different levels of skill, usually taught by people who have danced or studied professionally. There are studios geared to professional aspirations as well as those that are purely recreational. They can be quite expensive or comparable in price to Y's, parks and recreation departments, and adult education classes.

Racket clubs vary as much as fitness centers. Some are very exclusive and others welcome the public. You may find a local racket club that's not very different from the most luxurious health club, as well as one with only the bare necessities of courts, rackets, balls, and an instructor to give private and group lessons. There is wide variety in between. Each has its place for the right person. Prices vary according to the extent of facilities and personnel.

Country clubs are not always as elite or expensive as you might think. There are many affordable clubs. They may offer indoor and outdoor racket courts, pools, spas, golf courses, dining rooms, cocktail lounges, a calendar of social events, and an enjoyable group of people. Also, most have professional instructors available for private and group lessons. Country clubs vary in their facilities and price according to location and clientele.

The list of places to seek physical fitness goes on and on. Other options include schools in the martial arts, riflery and archery clubs, track clubs, and jogging organizations. To choose wisely, you need to determine the quality of these programs, in the same way you approach and tour a health club. Use available information and common sense to your advantage. Most places allow a free class or visit to help you make up your mind. Take advantage of this opportunity to be sure your aspirations are matched to the available offerings.

5

Breaking with Tradition: The Wilderness Challenge

WHILE TRADITIONAL SPORTS and games offer many opportunities for risk taking, wilderness experiences present entirely different challenges. Trading the familiarities of home for the risks of rocks, mountains, rivers, oceans, and deserts, women enter environments where they can live without interference from human technology.

The lack of intrusions is probably the strongest force that draws women from houses to tents and the open air. When telephones, taxis, and billboards are out of sight and mind, women are more able to get in touch with themselves and the earth, reestablishing a vital, strength-giving connectedness.

There's an intimate type of knowledge of the earth and universe that comes from walking on ground instead of pavement; catching a breeze rather than an icy blast from an air conditioner; swimming in lakes, rivers, or oceans instead of pools; hearing the wind move through grass and leaves; and seeing the face of the earth as it might have looked before cities were built. Even the stars seem closer without buildings and telephone lines to push them away and obscure their view.

Of course, all women may not view wilderness travel as romantically as this. "I hate taking all that gear and carrying it," said Vanessa. "It depresses my senses. A lot of energy goes into thinking about what I'm carrying. I feel like an animal." She thinks canoeing would be fun because she wouldn't have to carry everything on her back. Vanessa also resists what she terms "all that wilderness technology."

Vanessa is right about the technology. If it's bothersome, then it's no better than the technology that's left behind. On the other hand, technological advances have made lightweight gear possible, enabling many women to explore activities that weren't possible before. Any woman who wants to experience the joys and risks of the wilderness has to decide just how much energy she is willing to expend learning about, acquiring, and carrying equipment.

There may be trade-offs in terms of how long or how deeply a person immerses herself in the wilderness, but the beginnings of a wilderness experience may be as close as the outside door of one's home. Breathing fresh air instead of artificially heated or cooled air is a start. An awareness of pollutants in that air might force one to go where the air is fresher. The search, as always, begins inside oneself. It's a search for greater awareness of the natural things that are already a part of one's environment.

Not all environments are rich in easily recognizable elements of wilderness, but women can find any degree of wilderness they want or feel ready for. It's not even necessary to spend the night outdoors. Walking on a country road or a nature trail might be an ideal starting point. Camping out in a state park with telephones and other people nearby can be an end in itself or a logical transition to more remote wilderness areas.

TAKING RISKS

The farther one travels from civilization, the riskier such travel is. But each woman is accustomed to taking risks, even if she hasn't recognized them as such. If one considers the large risks already taken in one's life, then the risk of traveling far away from cities and people may not seem so dangerous.

Think of your own life over the past ten years. You have probably entered or left school, changed jobs, moved to a new place, gotten married or divorced, gone on a diet, learned a new skill or activity, given someone an honest opinion, worked for something you believe in, or dealt with an emergency or crisis.

How do you feel about having taken these risks? You probably wish you could be that efficient, strong, calm, or organized during the rest of your life. Or you don't really think of them as risks. You've likely been surprised to find that some of the things you consider to be commonplace are high-risk activities for someone else. If you've experienced these special times of strength and would like to experience that strength more often, or if you haven't but would like to, then you are not alone.

Michelle, a dancer, has recently taken a number of risks to be more involved in her dancing. She was not surprised at being accepted into a newly formed dance company, but she did have to take the large risk of quitting her job and moving to another, larger city to join the company. She did that without knowing in advance where she would live or what kind of work she might be able to find. She remembers the uncertainty of that time as being very scary.

When she made the initial transition to a totally new environment, she was rewarded by increased chances to dance. Her ability was recognized and applauded, and she felt good during and after performances. Rehearsals and classes were not always as pleasurable, however, and there was a month-long period when her job agency didn't have work for her.

Now she has a much stronger sense of what she is doing with her life. And for the first time she has reached that point having made her own decisions rather than using someone else's recommendations. She says that the process of figuring out what she wanted and needed to do and identifying what was hard for her and then doing it anyway has made her a lot stronger.

She feels that these kinds of risks are personal and that sometimes the riskiest part is simply making the decision to change. Some things seem like minor worries in retrospect, such as finding a place to live, but they aren't at the time. "It has made me stronger," she says. "I wouldn't be doing a lot of the things I'm doing now if I hadn't taken risks."

It is important for women to acknowledge and claim whatever risks they take. There are things they do each day that deserve a pat on the back. Each woman can begin by patting her own back and feeling good about taking risks.

Women take risks based on their own experiences. While one woman might take a risk by hiking fifty miles on the Appalachian Trail, another may do so by trying to decide if she is ready to spend the weekend at a public campground. Traveling a certain distance, short or long, is nothing in and of itself. What is crucial is promising yourself or others that you will reach a certain goal and then trying to meet those expectations. The risk of failure, either in your own eyes or the eyes of others, is a big one.

Risking disapproval by participating in a movement activity that is not common among peers or among women is another form of risk taking for women. Body building, playing rugby, rowing on a crew team, and whitewater kayaking are such activities. Women who engage in these types of activities may often find themselves on the defensive. It's difficult to explain one's enjoyment to someone who has other ideas about proper activities for women. Knowing that ten or twenty people are waiting for a chance to say "I told you so" is enough to deter many women from certain activities.

Besides claiming the risks they have already taken, women can gain confidence and enjoyment by creating risk-taking situations for themselves. Cindy will not be dissuaded from walking alone at night, whether for recreation or to run an errand. She thinks it's ridiculous not to be able to walk around in a town that's just as much hers as anyone else's. Cindy says that she likes to do bizarre, out-of-the-ordinary things because taking risks is what growing and learning are all about. Risks turn around any experience for her and give her a feeling of exhilaration. Wilderness experiences are noted for providing this type of feeling.

While taking risks may be exhilarating, it may also be painful and difficult. Four-year-old Kathi is learning to skate, but she is paying for the experience with scrapes and bruises to her knees, hands, and pride. Even experienced athletes sometimes overestimate their abilities or have a bad bounce. Just like Kathi, they may end up looking very foolish, being disappointed in themselves, or even becoming injured. A woman who is able to recognize the risks she is taking cannot avoid some bad feelings. But if she is aware of the risks, she can be more open and accepting of the consequences and be thrilled by the rewards.

Many women speak about growing and feeling strong and competent because of the risks they take. Risk-taking activities or situations vary, but women make such statements following activities such as rock climbing, canoeing, backpacking, and cross-country skiing.

When women enter a totally new and different movement environment, they may discover previously unknown skills and abilities within themselves. They are also less likely to have either high or low expectations for themselves in an unfamiliar environment. Not knowing what to expect makes it easier to do what needs to be done.

There is usually plenty of time to experiment with different ways of approaching an activity. A woman can immerse herself in the wilderness and travel at her own pace. She will have time to learn to trust the basic survival skills she already has, such as being alert to danger, communicating with others, and planning ahead for emergency situations. She can create a journey that's as difficult as she wants it to be. There's room to discover how something difficult can be enjoyable.

Wilderness travel can be challenging physically, mentally, and emotionally. Acquiring skills such as paddling a loaded canoe or finding a route by using a topographical map can make a person feel justifiably proud. Creating a challenging situation and meeting the challenge are a powerful source of feelings of self-worth that don't depend on the actions or reactions of other people.

Sitting on a riverbank or on the edge of a cliff, a woman can see so much more of her life in perspective and have time to reflect on it. She can be sensitive to more of the world around her. There is time, space, and quietude to feel her heart and lungs recovering from the climbing or paddling and to feel herself blending with the surroundings. The simple pleasures of cool water, warm sun, and the shades of colors in leaves become intensified.

Women can learn to carry that feeling of wholeness and wellness with them all the time, even when they are not in the wilderness. When they lose that feeling, they may try to regain it by going to nearby parks or playgrounds. Even half an hour free from the interference of human technology can help recharge their energy.

Understanding and acquiring the specialized equipment needed for backpacking, canoeing, skiing, or any other form of wilderness travel are often confusing tasks. Wilderness travel does not always necessitate spending a lot of money, but it is necessary to make wise and safe choices of equipment.

Any item you wear must be fitted correctly if it is to function as intended. Ill-fitting packs and boots can be especially troublesome on the trail. A paddle that is too long or too short results in extra work or inefficiently used energy. An inappropriate fuel for a stove could mean disaster.

Learning how to use and care for equipment properly takes time. Going on a journey with experienced wilderness travelers is one way to get an overall picture of what equipment is needed and how it is used. Reading books, magazines, and equipment catalogs is another way to learn about equipment. Knowledgeable salespeople in stores specializing in outdoor equipment are also helpful. It may be possible to borrow or rent equipment similar to what you think you want to purchase so you can see if it suits your needs.

Taking several short trips of increasing complexity and demand before your first major trip is advisable for learning about equipment and yourself in a wilderness situation. Day hikes and overnights in established campgrounds will help familiarize you with equipment and with your reactions to fatigue and stress. Always plan for the worst possible conditions, allowing more time than the trip should take. Having plenty of time and flexibility often prevents catastrophes.

Taking a class, going with friends, and using the services of a guide or outfitter are some ways of learning the small but important details of planning and executing a wilderness expedition. Many wilderness enthusiasts – professionals who get paid for the job, volunteers, or simply friends – are willing to take beginners on trips.

FINDING A LEADER

When trying something new, some women need the structure provided by an organized class or group. A group, and its leader in particular, can often provide the support, encouragement, and expertise needed to learn new activities. You might find classes of interest or leaders for wilderness excursions in the following areas:

- Local parks and recreation departments
- Continuing education centers affiliated with a college or university
- Local stores – sporting goods, camping, backpacking, outfitters; salespeople and bulletin boards
- Advertisements and classified sections in magazines devoted to outdoor activity
- Advertisements in women's magazines and journals
- Regular college courses
- Friends
- Women's centers
- Travel agencies
- Outdoor clubs and environmental groups (Appalachian Mountain Club, Sierra Club, and so on)

The kinds of wilderness experiences you get from these sources vary widely. The trips and guided tours offered through a travel agency may be very different from those offered by an outfitter at the edge of a wilderness area, but they may meet your needs. Throughout your inquiries, don't hesitate to express your concerns and to ask questions.

Sheila, a participant in trips led by others as well as a leader herself, has a lot of concerns about the type of leadership provided in movement activities for women. "I was once on a backpacking trip during which I was yelled at the entire time," she said, "because the only method the leader used to try to motivate certain other individuals was to yell at the whole group. I felt helpless and frustrated." As a leader, she has struggled with the issue of responsibility and realizes that being a good leader requires that she encourage others to express their needs and desires during the trip. Not knowing what others want or need sometimes makes it difficult to assist them.

What kind of leader is best and how does a woman find one? A lot of experience is not the only criterion. A wilderness leader should be able to teach a woman as much as possible about taking care of herself in the wilderness. Such teaching involves more than telling or showing. It involves an awareness of people's feelings and physical condition during the trip. Along with experience and empathy, a certain amount of knowledge is to be expected of leaders. In general, a more rugged, more remote, or less-used area requires more knowledge. In an emergency, remoteness makes the group even more dependent than usual on its own resources. In addition, knowing what equipment to select is an important pretrip consideration.

Leaders should also know first aid, rescue procedures (such as in water or on a rock face), map and compass reading, emergency survival, getting found, and any technical skills called for on a trip. The more knowledgeable and highly skilled a leader is, the more secure the group is. But everything is relative, and the amount of knowledge needed on a month-long trek in the Canadian wilderness is not the same as that needed for a weekend excursion on a well-marked, heavily traveled portion of the Appalachian Trail.

Experience and style in leading are other concerns. Many people who have spent lots of time in the wilderness have never taken the responsibility of introducing a beginner to their acquired skills and knowledge. They may have forgotten what it was like to be inexperienced, or they may have been so skillfully or naturally introduced that they feel the things they know have always been a part of them. If this is the case, their expectations and assumptions about what a beginner already knows may not match the reality. Novice participants must make their needs and their lack of understanding clear.

Some teachers simply tell you what to do and you do it; they may or may not provide the whole picture of what you are doing and why. Some leaders make sure you have a chance to try each skill, while others, for simplicity, assign certain individuals to certain tasks for the entire trip, such as building the fire, cooking the meals, reading the map, lighting the stove, and putting up the tents. Some leaders plan the entire trip, neither asking for nor expecting input from the participants. They will decide how fast to travel, when and where to rest and for how long, where and what to eat, where to put up tents, and so on. Others will not make any decisions without involving the total group in the process. Some leaders can and will vary their leadership style, depending on the apparent and expressed needs of the group. The leadership style you prefer depends on your own comfort and future purposes. If your ultimate goal is to be able to plan your own trips, then be sure to choose a leader who will give you a chance to try everything and who will allow you to be involved in planning.

A good leader will show overall concern for protecting the environment, often doing things a certain way to reduce human impact on the land. Environmentally sound wilderness travel places a high premium on leaving the land and water just as it was—no new fire scars, litter, noticeable latrines, or soap suds in the streams.

The kind of leader who is right for one woman may not be right for another. Use the following questions to think about how to match your learning style with someone else's leadership style.

- What am I least knowledgeable about?
- Do I like to be told what to do, to be given several choices, or to be allowed total freedom to explore on my own?
- Do I prefer to be given reasons for doing things in certain ways, or am I willing to trust someone I recognize as an expert?
- Do I customarily take responsibility for getting things organized, or do I like someone else to do it?
- What is the best way for me to learn new things?
- What responsibilities am I willing to give away?
- Do I want to have a part in the decision making? How much of a part?

There are no right or wrong answers to these questions. If you have trouble answering them, it may help to think back to your school experiences and the classes you enjoyed most and least. The methods of those teachers might give you clues.

When you have a good idea of how you prefer to be led, if at all, you can look for teachers and leaders who seem to meet your needs and preferences. Some are more willing than others to make changes. Don't hesitate to ask questions and try to establish a dialogue. Most leaders are grateful for interaction.

Some organizations offer leadership and wilderness experiences for groups of women only. These classes and trips, which vary in difficulty and length, can be an enjoyable way for women to learn many of the necessary skills for wilderness travel. Traveling with mixed groups can be rewarding too, but some women feel that the sharing of learning, leading, and decision making can be particularly gratifying in all-women groups. There is not much difference among groups in *what* is done – there is never a question in either group whether women can do all activities – but there is a difference in *how* things are done.

Frequently, a man's introduction to wilderness is through hunting, fishing, scouts, or the armed services. These experiences are often taken for granted among males and often involve a lot of competition. If men go hunting with someone, they can swap stories and have a common ground to communicate what to do in the woods.

Women rarely bring the same number of experiences or the same role models to wilderness experience as men do. They don't always share a common background for communication about the wilderness. Because they are beginners, everything seems new and unrelated to the skills they use at home, even if it isn't. Friction can occur when beginners with one set of assumptions enter a new, wild environment with experienced travelers who are not sensitive to their needs.

In women's groups, hard times, good times, leadership, and decision making are all shared experiences, sometimes in very intense ways. These times can leave women feeling stronger and more in touch with themselves and each other. In mixed groups, these feelings are not always shared. People seem less willing or able to work together. The dominant feelings are often of triumph and gratefulness that hard times are over, and the feelings of communication, strength, self-awareness, and self-knowledge are downplayed.

This is not to suggest that participation in wilderness experiences with male leaders and group members should be avoided, or that women-only groups are always ideal. Every group has its own unique blend of skills and personalities. Women need to be aware of what they want from an experience and do everything possible to get it. Talk about what you want beforehand with the leader and group members. If your companions don't seem to understand, try to find different companions for your next experience. Form your own group. The skills and sensitivities needed to be comfortable in the wilderness, or in any movement setting, are available to all women.

GROUP CHALLENGES

Dorian told of one all-women's canoe trip in Canada in which elements from several settings and individual characteristics of the other group members had become blended in her memory. Eleven women went on a three-week adventure sponsored by a women-only outfitting and educational organization. The trip included paddling in whitewater and was advertised to attract women with a strong sense of adventure, preferably with some wilderness or paddling experience.

The journey was preceded by a day and a half of working together to pack food, prepare equipment, and plan an alternate route because there had been forest fires in the area in which they had intended to travel. There were far more rewards than difficulties reported on this trip because each person contributed toward daily tasks, helped solve major problems, and met the demands of minor and major crises and emergencies. Dorian recalled some instances of traveling on the river that illustrate both group problem solving and individual thrills and special times:

"There had been an accident up ahead with one of the canoes. Once Nadia and I got closer, we could see Lori and Robyn's half-capsized canoe pinned against a submerged rock. Water was pouring into and over the bow. Robyn, in the stern, was fighting to keep her paddle in the fast-moving water to prevent further capsizing." Dorian remembered watching while Lori carefully climbed out of the bow into the breathtakingly cold Canadian water. Struggling against current and rocks she freed the canoe, which shot away from her, with a surprised Robyn paddling furiously.

There were many rocks and it was getting dark, so Robyn and the canoe were immediately lost from sight. Nadia started walking toward Lori with Dorian following. Half wading for a while, then walking and jumping across the rocks, Lori made her way toward them. She was soaked. Even though Robyn had successfully negotiated the rest of the rapids, Dorian wondered how the rest of the group would ever make it through.

Since the shore was too rocky or steep to carry the gear and canoes, and the center of the river had already claimed one canoe, they decided to guide the canoes through and around the rocks by lining them – attaching ropes to both ends to guide them. It took a lot of teamwork to maneuver the long canoes, and they ended up having to wade in the water beside them, carefully searching the bottom for footholds among the rocks.

With amusement, Dorian explained how she had always enjoyed rock-hopping "and I was just beginning to find some enjoyment in the underwater version, when I suddenly found myself up to my nose in water. Thanks to my life jacket and the instinctive actions of my feet, I didn't stay there long. As we continued our journey in what had become moonlight, we had to lift and tug the canoes as often as we were letting them float. By the time we finished, it was dark. We were all wet, tired, and hungry."

Dorian mentioned that working together in many situations like this helped the group members to trust themselves, both as individuals and as a group. They learned to use all of the group's resources in solving problems, listening to everyone's viewpoint. The new strength in their bodies from the days of paddling and portaging was very rewarding. Dorian admitted spending quite a lot of time in front of the first real mirror she found upon returning to civilization.

The pace of their traveling varied according to their needs and desires. But as the end of the trip neared, they all felt a certain tension about leaving the river and the rhythm they had established. "During evening conversations," Dorian said, "we would talk about who we were and why we were on the river. We all, even the leaders, had other jobs in the city.

We were teachers, students, medical workers, office managers, an artist, a researcher, and other types of workers. Some of us liked our jobs, and others didn't. Some of us had paddled in the wilderness before, and others hadn't. One had never paddled at all, and very few had paddled in whitewater. We shared a sense of longing for the wholeness that comes with having time, quiet, and support to find our own rhythms and best ways of doing things. To varying degrees, we were searching for adventure, risk, challenge, and new definitions of ourselves."

Risk and challenge had different meanings for each member. There was the risk of novices having to trust more experienced paddlers until their own skills were developed. Everyone faced the risk of serious injury or illness in a very remote and inaccessible area. The prospect of three intimate weeks with a group of unfamiliar women was probably equally threatening.

Perhaps the biggest risks were the unknown elements of weather, terrain, and unexpected happenings. Since the originally proposed route had been eliminated because of major forest fires, Dorian and her companions were well aware that any number of calamities might occur. What if they got lost? What if they couldn't cope with an emergency?

Hour by hour and minute by minute there were individual risks to take and decisions to make. Should Dorian paddle these rapids or portage her gear on land? Could Lori safely tote a smaller pack in addition to the large one she already had? Nadia would really like to climb along that cliff for a better view, but would she be able to get down? Could Robyn get over that log while portaging the canoe, or should she put the canoe down and wait for help? From their conversations, Dorian knew that each woman encountered many moments of personal risk and challenge. Isabel found she could indeed carry a canoe, and Jean discovered that paddling in the stern was actually fun. Each woman learned a lot about trusting her own intuition.

The trip was intense not only in terms of solving problems. There were many ecstatic times too. The most memorable moments for Dorian were when she learned to paddle in the fast water without overturning or crashing into the rocks. Learning to choose a safe route meant learning how to read the water and how to decide, instantly at times, where to paddle. Learning to execute the route she had chosen meant learning to wield the paddle effectively, using the strength of her whole body.

Remembering one particular set of rapids, Dorian explained, "The river was so wide that there were enough options for each canoe to choose a different route. Isabel and I received a bit of complimentary teasing about our 'elegant' choice. We headed straight for the biggest standing waves, the ones we knew didn't have rocks hiding behind them, and we bounced gloriously up and down throughout the run, enjoying the speed of our motion, the jolts from bouncing, and the soaking we got from the spray. I still get chills of pleasure when I think of that!"

The group as a whole, Dorian remarked, became quite good at working together and taking a great deal of open pleasure in it. Unfailingly, one person's high energy was always available to fill in for another's low. Knowing that returning home would make it hard to hold on to the more natural rhythms that had been developing, the group worked toward an understanding. Obligations to jobs, households, and a much larger circle of acquaintances would make the women at least a little clock-conscious again. The close ties they had developed with their journeymates would be disrupted, if not broken entirely. They talked about that with one another, doing what they could to help one another make the transition.

They also knew they had been changed by their experiences and that the person who was returning would not be the same one who had left three weeks before. As much as they longed to be home with the people closest to them, the adventurers anticipated that their loved ones would not understand what had happened and how they had changed. They themselves didn't fully understand. One thing they had learned was their ability to recognize and solve problems. They were not totally unequipped to handle the new set of challenges at home.

Now that Dorian is back in the city, she often remembers her experiences on that trip and many others. She uses the memories to strengthen her good feelings about herself and to pick herself up when she's feeling down. Knowing that she has attempted difficult tasks and accomplished them makes her more able to do the hard things she has to do now. Even though taking risks is not always fun or smooth, she treasures what she has learned. When she looks back, she is surprised at how easily she remembers the physical strength she gained and forgets the sore muscles that paved the way. "It's strange to remember more about the songs we sang than the bugs that tortured us. My overall feelings are so positive and joyous!"

Dorian believes that her travels into the wilderness never end. They are always with her, providing powerful knowledge of her own strength and worth. In addition, there is always one more horizon to cross, another landscape from which to view the setting sun and rising moon. "I always return from the wilderness with a more complete and integrated self than the one I entered with," said Dorian. "Somehow, just the daily tasks of eating, traveling, and sleeping take on an added dimension of wholeness when they are done in a natural setting. I have never regretted any of the things I've sampled, even though I consider myself lucky to have survived some of them. I look forward to learning more about canoeing because that seems to get you deeper into the wilderness in a shorter amount of time."

GOING ALONE OR AT ALL

There may be women who have a strong desire to spend time in the wilderness but wish to do so alone rather than as a group member. Solitude is one of the salient features of wilderness travel. Women who wish to go alone, or even with one other person, take a larger risk than those who travel in groups. Because of this, they need to take more elaborate safety precautions.

A woman who sets out alone must be in shape for the kind of traveling she has chosen and be skillful in the specialized techniques required. She must know how to take care of herself in emergency situations. She has probably had a lot of experience living in the wilderness and is able to make sound judgments about such things as map reading, whether to attempt a certain route, where to make camp, reading the signs that foretell the weather, what natural things are safe to eat, and anything involving her own abilities and limitations. Her planning and preparation must be thorough, especially related to food and the availability of water. She should leave a proposed itinerary with someone she knows as well as with any authorities who need to know her approximate whereabouts.

Most women can appreciate accounts of the benefits of wilderness travel, though not all will choose to participate. Those who do feel a tug of desire to try it for themselves may have fears and doubts about entering the wilderness or engaging in other risk-taking activities.

The monologue varies from person to person, but it runs something like this: "I'm not sure I can make it—I'm not in very good shape. I'll never be able to carry that pack all day! I'm afraid I'll hold the others back. How will we get the canoes across the portage? Aren't there snakes (bears, mountain lions)? If I can't take my electric blanket I'm not going. It's too cold (hot, damp). You've got to be kidding— sleep on the ground?! Is the water safe? I've never built a fire, much less cooked on one. I'm allergic to bee stings. Did you see *Easy Rider*? What if someone gets hurt? What if it rains? What if we get lost?" The worries and fears are not imaginary.

A woman who wants to try a wilderness experience or other new activity in spite of her concerns is allowing herself a chance to grow, learn, and enjoy life in very special ways. If a woman wants to create her own experience rather than depend on a leader or organization, her best approach is simply to become as knowledgeable as possible. When a woman is faced with a new and frightening situation, it is important that she carefully separate facts and realities from suppositions and imaginings. With accurate information about the situation, she can then plan and execute a course of action. If a woman is willing to introduce herself to the wilderness gradually and if she prepares herself by knowing as much as she can about the risks involved and how to meet them, then she can create an enjoyable and worthwhile experience.

6
Selfful Experiences– Special Moments

THE ABSURD, OFFBEAT, spontaneous, unusual, silly, inconceivable, and surprising moments of one's life can be very thrilling. Those times of discovering the unexpected can offer both a striking change from the everyday and a reason to keep seeking and exploring new possibilities. One who does not experience or recall these moments may not be recognizing one's potential strengths and talents.

As grand as these moments appear, women tend to overlook them when seeing themselves as movers. For all the tales of horror told of gym classes and other activities, there are very few stories circulating that reveal the good, special times in the same settings. For some women, this is a realistic balance – many instances where forgetting would be more desirable than reliving. But while the worth of these special times cannot easily counteract the horrible times, many women give a lot of weight to the negative movement experiences and disavow the positive ones. It's easy to come up with a memory of being clumsy, awkward, or out of place, but it takes a determined effort to remember pleasing and enjoyable moments. This doesn't have to be the case.

The tug that pulls women away from organized sports and other movement activities also makes them remark about the futility of retaining a firm attachment to such activities. Even women who see themselves as having some ability to derive pleasure from moving are apt to make negative remarks about their own performances and capabilities. The favorable, positive times have been overshadowed by moments that were unenjoyable and negative.

A book about feeling uncomfortable and out of place while moving does not have to be written for women. Women do it for themselves. Each woman is a great storyteller of being a misfit as a mover. The task is easy – almost too easy, like talking about the weather. A narrow understanding takes the place of real knowledge. Tales of the gym relate only a fraction of what it's like to be a female who moves. The rest of the story needs to be uncovered and spoken about too. Women have yet to reveal to themselves the multiplicity of worthwhile experiences available to them while moving. Why not start now?

ELIMINATING OBSTACLES

A major obstacle to moving is the unfounded opinion that one has to be highly skilled to gain much pleasure from an activity. If this were true, there would be little hope for many women to be appreciably satisfied. Regardless of your level of skill in whatever activity you've tried or are thinking of trying, the activity has its own chances for providing you with surprising, unusual, and satisfying experiences. This is as true for the highly skilled female athlete who is trying out a novel activity as it is for a woman who is returning to an activity after many years of inactivity. The joys are reachable for all women who move.

There is no denying that events you would rather not repeat come mixed with the ones you would willingly redo again and again. As a mover, you encounter both. When you choose to ignore the uplifting times and highlight only the catastrophes, however, you find you're unable to move.

If you could expect to feel good when you moved, and if you could recognize, capture, and sustain a euphoric moment, that could be a starting point when reasoning failed. If your memories include a host of pleasurable experiences, you can use them as springboards to motivate you to remain active.

Violet, for example, struggled to recall favorable moments. She said she is "a nonsports person. I just happened to race in a couple of races. It isn't sport. It's similar to ironing. It's just something I do." When she wanted to, Violet kept up a regular training schedule for running, completed many races including a half-marathon, and seriously considered running a marathon. At other times, running doesn't enter her thoughts. "I accept that I'm relatively sedentary," Violet said. "If I'm not doing it at the moment, I'm really not interested. A certain amount of obsession is necessary to maintain the sport. I don't like the commitment of having to do it every day. It gets old."

In thinking back to her childhood, Violet recalls what an awful time she had in gym class because she never seemed to do anything right. She talked about this, with one important addition: "P.E. teachers loathed me. They just could not deal with me. But I always did like gymnastics." Gymnastics, the one activity she had enjoyed in school, had been forgotten in favor of the distasteful experiences.

When asked how the special times of sports participation fit in her life, she said, "I guess I don't know how to apply them. I'm not sure it's worth that effort to have the fun. I don't see the daily applications in my life." Remembering more of the good times may help her make more useful connections between herself and movement.

Violet hasn't totally given up on running. The time restrictions of having a full-time job and caring for a young daughter by herself make the thought of running unpleasant, as does her feeling that she is overweight and her dislike of hearing rude remarks from passing motorists. But, she noted, "They were good times. They were fun. A lot of the time I spent alone was real nice and real healing. One reason I'm considering getting back to it is to get some time alone."

Like so many other women, Violet is much more aware of the unappealing sides of being active and has few ways of resolving the negative memories that pull at her and keep her from running. The experiences that might add to her feelings of enjoyment have either been forgotten or brushed aside. She hasn't discovered how to strike a balance.

The key is to make room for satisfying yourself – knowing when the moment feels right and keeping a hold on it by forming a vivid memory. Once the favorable memories begin accumulating, it's much easier to understand how and why moving is a part of your life and well-being. From there, it's a matter of making the most of the better experiences, taking an active part in increasing the odds that they will occur.

There is no need to block out the bad memories. They can be used too. When viewed in perspective, they can reveal why a situation didn't work. Instead of avoiding the unpleasant, make the most of it. No doubt, such situations will happen. Prepare yourself with a direct, productive way of dealing with what at first appears to be something you'd rather turn your back on.

Rather than separating movement experiences into isolated instances of good-bad, positive-negative, enjoyable-unenjoyable, and so on, try to overlap and integrate them. Make them work together. When you're not completely satisfied with the activity you're doing, change it. Don't do laps around the track when you'd rather see new scenery as you run. If your routine was devised based on only the latest ideas in physical training, maybe a bit of psychological understanding is called for. The best movement program is the one that fits you best; you help determine that.

If everything is going along as well as can be, use the positive feelings this generates to influence the more negative times. Keep the recollection handy. Give yourself a lift by instantly thinking back to the last satisfying movement experience you had. Double-faulting on a serve isn't half as bad when you remember your last ace – instead of your last error.

Once you label a movement experience "good" or "bad," it's hard ever to see it differently. The ability to view it from another angle becomes stifled. Look on your own experiences as adaptable and changeable. The line goes that apples and oranges don't mix. But if, instead, one wants a unique fruit juice, the two can be blended. Avoid the temptation to unnecessarily categorize. Stay flexible.

Gail was in a situation where she took the seemingly good with the bad and made it better. She was on her first canoe trip into northern Minnesota. The surroundings were primitive and often frightening. They forced her to depend on herself and demanded an extra amount of her attention. But Gail not only coped with her unfamiliar surroundings, she also had one of the most exciting experiences of her life.

"I felt scared a lot of the time," she said, "because I wasn't sure that my instincts were right about certain things. I would hear a noise, and I could either decide it was a bear or just lay real still and try to let it pass. There were a lot of decisions I had to make that I just wasn't sure were the right decisions at the time.

"That's what gave me such a high feeling. I was rewarded when I would make the right decision. I was really, really scared, but then after the crisis or the incident passed, I felt I had done the right thing. And then I would get a little higher . . .

"I'm always kind of scared at first. Usually it's something that I want to do and I'll be afraid to do it because I'm afraid I might fail. But if I push myself and say, 'Go ahead and do it. You want to do it. Don't let your fears stop you,' those are the times I get high feelings. I have to be afraid of it first, or I don't get that high feeling."

The irony of some of the best movement experiences one can have is that elements such as fear, cold, frustration, exhaustion, and stress become useful. There's a new twist that makes them desirable. A challenge is created, rather than a situation to avoid or to flee from.

Gail overcame a fearful situation and reaped the benefits. The result was an increased sense of self-worth and, she said, "I have a great deal of confidence and love, not only for myself but for everything around me — the water, the trees, the people. Everything is synchronized. Everything is flowing. That's the best word I can use for it. Everything just flows."

WHAT THE EXPERIENCE IS

Experiences like Gail's come in many forms. Runners experience a so-called high, and downhill skiers have been known to sparkle with excitement during and after a successful run. Racquetball courts, weight rooms, lacrosse fields, golf courses, or softball diamonds can be the site of a meaningful, unifying, and long-lasting experience. Each one leaves its own impression and affects you in a different way. Neither your skill level nor the activity determines the effect. You do. The degree of your involvement in the situation dictates the outcome.

This type of experience is recognized in movement-related fields and in other areas. Psychology calls it a peak experience, parapsychology calls it psi, Eastern philosophy classifies it as satori, and theology calls it ecstasy. Instead of drawing these experiences together with a common bond, the tendency is to separate them by pointing out the differences among the labeled experiences. Strict definitions of experience decrease the odds of a person's having such an experience. More people are eliminated by the definitions than are included. Active women are no exception. Validating a euphoric experience can be difficult. Not knowing what to call it, how to talk about it, or what it takes to have such an experience can present problems. A woman bowling for the second time in her life may question her senses when she is unexpectedly euphoric after converting a split. The moment may feel so right, yet the bowler who doesn't understand what's happening may disregard the whole experience. If there's nothing to compare it to, the moment may be lost.

When movement experiences bring on euphoric feelings, new insights, and a sense of oneness with the surroundings we call them *selfful experiences*. They act like a filter through which perceptions can be seen and organized. A person forms an awareness of her potentials now and for the future. These selfful experiences are special and important, enlivening the everyday and making life more worthwhile. One is enriched and fulfilled by the connections between oneself and one's surroundings.

A female backpacker said it's like "trying to drink in everything that's happening. I remember thinking I'd like to drink all this in, whether it's a sight or an event or the good feelings I have when I know that I can do something that I didn't know I could do before."

Another woman described it by saying, "It's a centered feeling, yet it extends all over my body. Every part of my body is in motion. It's different from anxiety or tenseness. It's a relaxed flow." She added, "It gives me a sense of power and makes me feel ten feet tall. It puts me on a high plane."

No one is excluded from having selfful experiences. You are the sole judge of how meaningful an experience is. Stay focused on how you're feeling and what you need to do to make the moment even more special. The idea may seem new when looking at yourself as a mover, but you've probably done this several times throughout your life – even in movement activities. By playing an active rather than a passive role, you will see new options.

"If you can fantasize it happening," one woman said, "it can happen. It's a spontaneous thing. You could have imagined yourself doing it before and felt good about it, but all of a sudden, out of nowhere, when you least expect it, it happens. You're just real excited. It's not scared, nervous, but an internally high, emotional level. Happiness."

MOVING WITH THE EXPERIENCE

There may be some confusion about how much control a woman can have over a selfful movement experience. Words like *intent*, *making it happen*, and *expecting* seem to contradict *letting go*, *flowing*, and *floating*. The first group of words implies that one has an active part to play, while the latter suggests passivity. Actually, both apply to selfful experiences.

Wanting something to happen is a powerful force. There's energy, striving, and plenty of forward motion. Intensity and desire are present; maybe you'll get what you want, or maybe you won't. Still, you go after it, and when and if you get it, you need to stop pushing and start relaxing and taking in what you've achieved. Any resistance you feel has to disappear. This is where active changes to passive. But the initial desire and envisioning of a goal lead to the orgasmlike selfful experience. It's the active striving that gets the ball rolling.

Your control of the situation is a balance of what you seek and what you do once you reach your goal. If you don't put enough emphasis on wanting something, or if you don't relax once you've attained the goal, you haven't used the necessary control. Work at it. Play with it. Put yourself in situations where you can alter the intensity of an activity. When you sense you're becoming united with the surroundings and a euphoric feeling starts filtering in, allow the sensation to affect you. Try not to resist. Let yourself expand with the feelings. Take in what you can, even though it may be strange or novel. Afterward you can sort through what happened, but while you're selffully experiencing, enjoy the ride. Take an active, controlling part in these important moments that are yours as a woman in motion.

Elizabeth did. She was playing the infield during an evening softball game: "I had the lights shining right down on my head. It's a real strange feeling. The batter is very close to you and there's something about the lights and the way the field is set up that makes it seem much farther away than it actually is. At times I've been really tense and hyped up about what was going on and I felt like all these people are playing this game around me and here I am, not quite feeling like it's real . . .

"If I stop and think about what I'm doing instead of just experiencing it, games are really pretty stupid. That's the only time I've felt that way – when I'm sitting and waiting for things to happen. All of a sudden it just sort of hits me that this doesn't seem very real. Why are we here? What am I doing here? At the same time, it's exciting. I don't feel that way unless I'm hyped up and ready to play." Elizabeth's active waiting works for her in a setting where the structured activity makes little sense.

CUEING AND RECALLING

In order to remember your own selfful moments, think back over your movement history. Make an effort to recall those special moments. This may take some searching on your part because you've likely filed many of these memories in an inaccessible spot. Dust off as many recollections as you can of movement activities in your life. Pay attention to the remembrances that come back to you first and to those that try to elude you. That will help reveal why you haven't thought about them in a long time. Don't leave out the memories you already enjoy thinking back to. Use everything you have.

Find ways to cue yourself. Think of the times you earned a ribbon, a medal, or a pat on the back. Try to recall the details of riding your bicycle or skating for the first time. At some time, you've probably thrown and caught a ball, climbed up a tree, or vaulted a fire hydrant. There may have been an outfit you played in that you never wanted to outgrow. Watching someone else do an activity you wished you could do might be a memory worth exploring.

In the past year, there have been moments that were best for you as a mover. You can repeat or build on those good times. You also might have prevented yourself from having a good time because you anticipated feeling awkward or clumsy. If you were presented with that same situation now, you could change the circumstances to suit you better and to actively enhance the movement situation. Recall those good feelings when you start losing sight of the fun you're having.

Know that you're able to have an infinite supply of selfful moments.

"I can look back and remember having all these feelings," one woman said, "but I never could understand them until I achieved some body awareness in the past four or five years. I never really thought much about physical sensations and what they mean and how they're integrated into who you are. But once I started getting an awareness and it was okay to know my body was feeling good, I came to understand that these sensations are integrated into who you are emotionally and psychologically."

Once she allowed herself to recognize the sensations she had been denying, she had "so much energy I didn't express elsewhere that I could express in basketball. It involved running, body control, and coordination. You get immediate feedback about your success or failure. You either block a shot, or you don't. It's a real challenge to develop that skill."

Recalling past experiences can be fun in itself, but you can also use past experiences to stimulate a pleasurable feeling that can stay with you for a long time. By discovering how integral they are to your well-being, you open up new dimensions. You find you have been, and will continue to be, a woman in motion. It's no longer a matter of beginning now, at whatever age you are. You have rejoined and reconnected a part of yourself that had been in the shadows. Recollections are a way to feel yourself in harmony. Remember, they're as free, obtainable, and ever-present as any experience you've ever had or will have.

"I guess I do think about them when I need them," Adele said about her experiences playing softball. "Being forty-one, sometimes I think about playing ball. Those were the days. Usually I get a mellow, pleasant feeling from it and nostalgia for the things I don't do anymore . . .

"I was able to go to tournaments with all the big kids, traveling four hundred miles. We always won. I think we lost three games in three years, except for tournaments. We felt hot and important and we looked sharp. And that, yes, is very pleasant, and it was at the time, too . . .

"We would go to tournaments in those big ballparks with lights and stands full of people. I was scared. I wasn't old enough to handle it. I know now that all I have to do is concentrate on the ball. But in those days, if I was going to screw up, that's when it happened. The world tournament, for example, was scary. I was sixteen. But I got over it . . .

"After playing a ball game, I was as tired as can be. But it was a good kind of tired, having done my best . . . We never slept after a ball game. We talked all night until we were too tired to relive the game anymore. I suppose sometimes I'm not aware of that high until after it's over. It's an energy thing, like being involved and working hard at something and then realizing later that you were on your feet for twelve hours and never got tired."

Adele and the other women we interviewed were asked to use a scale of one to ten to rate how they felt on the day they were interviewed, on a typical day, and during a selfful experience. The selfful experiences were the obvious high scorers, sometimes being rated beyond ten. Recalling such joyous times of the past can influence the present.

"You're generally as happy as you make up your mind to be," Adele said. "I really believe that. And that's a high. It's just a question of realizing all the terrific things that there are and stopping and catching them. Even two days go up to at least a five, if you can do that."

WILLING SELFFUL EXPERIENCES

Becoming more familiar with what selfful movement experiences are and learning how to recall them and use them to feel more alive can be very valuable. So can making an effort willfully to have this type of experience. Instead of daydreaming about what it would be like to live a euphoric, fulfilling moment, act on the urge. See what you can do to live the experience, not just fantasize about it.

Like anything else that seems new and different, your initial attempts may not be as successful as you would like them to be. It takes a while to become efficient at a novel activity.

A bit of skepticism may hold you back, too. It may be hard at first to believe you have a part to play in initiating a selfful experience. When you think it over, however, the idea starts making more sense.

Several of the women who were interviewed were asked if they could will a selfful experience. The overwhelming response was no. When asked if they had actually tried to initiate the experience, most women said no. Without ever having attempted to willfully bring about the experience, these women concluded it was impossible to do. The consensus was "I cannot will a selfful experience because I have never willed one before." This is like assuming you can't complete a marathon because you've never entered one. If this were true, then these desirable selfful experiences would be left up to chance. If one didn't have them, one could do nothing about it. But maybe something can be done.

Having power over oneself can be a scary feeling. A woman who defines her own path and invests her energy in ways she sees fit has a lot of responsibility. Managing one's resources and making decisions can be both rewarding and tiring. The good times in the life of a woman in motion have a place right here. By taking the initiative to want to feel especially good when involved in movement activities, each woman assumes more responsibility for seeing that it happens.

This power to favorably control and give direction need not be feared. Consider it a gift to yourself, free of charge. All you have to do is be willing to move when you feel the urge — acting on it instead of fantasizing or ignoring it. Then, get as much as you can out of the movement experience. When you feel things are falling into place or you can make them fall into place, willfully reach for the best sensations possible. Take the power you have to feel yourself as a moving woman. Settle into the moment. Affirm that you can and do like what you're feeling and that it's rightfully yours. You can willfully, intentionally repeat or find a similar moment.

The women we interviewed unknowingly gave hints of what it might take to do what they think can't be done. They indicated that a selfful experience could be willed by finding another way to actively try, being in the right situation, making something good even better, or knowing what mood will work. All of these are important and can be the difference between a moment becoming special or being forgotten.

One woman said she can will such an experience "to a certain extent. I plan to do certain things that are going to make me feel like that: floating rivers, some sports, being in a swimming race. If I were near Lake Superior, I'd be in it a lot. As far as swimming, racing is just an incredible high because it does things physiologically that I don't get in any other way, except maybe running. After swimming, I feel light-headed and completely worked out. That's a real rush."

Elizabeth uses a different technique to stir her involvement: "Just focusing on whatever it is and reliving it in my mind. Thinking about it so that I feel like I'm back in that space again and feeling that original excitement. I mentally conjure up all the good details in the situation."

The uses of recall and will are closely aligned. With access to recollections, women can will memorable movement experiences and comprehend what they mean. Also, if a woman makes a determined effort to have a selfful experience, she can recall the moment in the future. Recalling and willing selfful movement experiences are as important as the experiences themselves.

UNEXPECTED REWARDS

Not all efforts will yield what you desire, but movement activities have an infinite potential to be satisfying and worthwhile. You must simply explore them with a playful and determined attitude. Sometimes pushing yourself will be what you need, and other times simply doing what you're doing or easing up will be the necessary energy investment. Listen to yourself. You'll learn to sense what's right. While you're listening, don't be surprised if you come across both ironic and humorous impressions. Effort is rewarded in many ways.

One of Violet's running experiences points this out. In one race Violet was running along at a good pace. It was so good that she was the first person to near the finish line. As she ran toward it, she noticed a strange blockade and ducked under it – she had run under the winner's tape. Violet said the reason she didn't go through it was "I didn't know what it was."

Ironies abound in movement experiences. The common sensations are inevitably mixed in with the unexpected and unanticipated. Regardless of how familiar situations seem, there is always room for a new twist. Taking them humorously, at least in retrospect, is one way to deal with them.

Janet wasn't very active in sports in high school, but she began making up for it during college. A member of a farming family, she had lived too far from the town to be able to participate in school sports. During the first few weeks of college, she began playing flag football. The experience she had might have devastated some women, but Janet described it as a selfful one.

"We were playing a new defensive pattern. I was right defensive end, and my friend Marie was playing left defensive end. Big D. Our coach was quarterback and we were practicing a new defensive position. I was so determined to get that ball from him, and Marie was real determined to get the ball too. Before I knew it, we were both lying on the ground . . .

"I was ready to get up and go play ball again because I'm not a quitter. Everyone's yelling, 'Lay down.' 'Why?' I asked. All of a sudden I felt this trickle going down my head. 'What happened?' They said, 'Oh, you just bashed your head open.' I said, 'How could I do that? We only hit heads. That's not possible.' 'Yes it is. You've got sharp bones up there.'

"So everybody ran around, getting rags and this and that. They finally got a car and hauled me off to the hospital. I'd never been in an emergency room before – I'd never really been in a hospital – and here I was, playing football, banged up . . .

"Marie was about ready to pass out, and she didn't even get hurt like I did. I had gashed my right eye and they had to shave my eyebrow off. I wound up with two huge black eyes. The doctor gave me medicine to spread the swelling from my right eye over to my left eye. The funny thing is that I've always wanted a black eye, just to see what it was like. Well, I got a little more than I wanted . . .

"Afterward I was more cautious about playing, because I didn't want to break the stitches open again. It took me a long time to get rid of the swelling. Once my eyebrow grew back, the nurse made me swab it with peroxide. That bleached it out, so there I was with a blond eyebrow and a brown one."

This wasn't the only situation in which Janet ventured far from the norm. In a later selfful experience, she was confronted with something novel during a softball game. While retelling what happened, Janet was able to see the situation with humor.

"I had gotten on base and had miraculously made my way to third. The first time I'd ever been on third. I didn't know what it looked like. I stole from second to third, because the pitcher was really bad, and she was walking us all. They kept switching pitchers, and all they could do was walk us.

"Then someone got a hit, and I came running in. For some reason the ump called it. He said go back to the base. So I went back to third again. And then there was a wild pitch, so I chanced it. I was about halfway between third and home and I realized, 'Oh my gosh. The catcher's got the ball. I've got to slide.'

"I had never slid in my life, so I said, 'This has got to be it.' I closed my eyes and slid. All I knew was that there was enough dirt to plow eighty acres of ground. There was dirt all over the place. The ump yelled, 'Safe!' and I was underneath the catcher. I didn't even get dirty. But I had never done anything like that, and it was such a good feeling . . .

"I put us ahead one run. The crowd was going wild. People I didn't even know were yelling my name. Everybody came up, grabbing me, hugging me, slapping me on the back . . ."

Feelings of excitement swept through Janet. "I felt really, really good because I knew I had the potential to do something, but I just wasn't given the chance. So when this happened, I thought, All right. Now I finally had my chance to show somebody that I can play ball. We all have our bad nights, but at least I finally got a chance to do something like that . . .

"It was a beautiful slide. I have big old buns, and I had shorts on. I didn't skin anything up. I had asked my friend Julie one day at work, 'How do you slide?' She said, 'Grab a handful of dirt so that you won't want to grab when you're sliding.' So for some reason, I thought of that when I saw I had to slide. I closed my fist. I didn't really have any dirt in my hands, but I kept them closed, and I just went down on my butt and slid.

"Then, when I got home that night, I practiced sliding, on my floor, in front of the mirror. Let's have another replay of that. What did it look like, you know? So that's what I was doing. But I haven't had a chance to make a slide like that since. It gave me a high feeling to do it."

Laughing at and with yourself is a good approach to recapturing those forgotten memories. Ann thinks back quite frequently to a softball experience that took place a dozen years ago. She was playing first base and was a fairly good player. A pitched ball was met with the crack of a bat, and she saw instantly that the ball was about to fly between her and second base. With action more than thought, she propelled herself up and over toward the ball, sticking her gloved hand out as far as humanly possible. When she landed, she found the ball wedged in her glove. What a glorious feeling. She had put the player out and made a terrific play.

She brushed her pants off and still retained a good, tingling feeling about her performance. It didn't take long before a different batter connected with the ball, sending it to that same magic place as before. In a moment, Ann reached for the ball, knowing full well that history was repeating itself. Well, almost. She did make a great stabbing try. And she did land in the dirt. But the ball happened to be at least ten feet farther away from her than it had been the first time. Ann said it felt good to be flying through the air. She was totally embarrassed at the time but now she can look back at the experience with humor and understanding.

TELL SOMEONE

After selfful movement experiences happen, recall them and then verbally share the experience with others. Start developing a language to translate those overwhelming feelings into words and gestures. Let them out. Express your feelings about the experiences. Give them another dimension.

Take the time to understand how you value the experience. You've had it and recalled it, and now make the effort to uncover what it means and how it fits into your sense of the woman you are. Convey the experience to someone else and see what an impact it makes on you and the other person.

Relating experiences that seem to have no words to describe them is frustrating enough, but add to that an unsureness of yourself as a woman in motion and you've got a difficult task. Think of how many times and in what different ways you have expressed your happiness to someone else. Did you get the message across on the first try? Because selfful experiences are so powerful to you, you might assume that the first person you tell your euphoric tale to will understand you and feel as happy as you do about it. Quite unlikely. Someday this may be the case, but for now you'll probably have to summon up both concentration and patience to get your message across.

Knowing how and why the experience influenced you can help you focus on what you need to say, even when the other person does not appear to be catching on. Your very strong feelings do not guarantee that your listener knows how to pick up your cues, blatant or not.

The selfful movement experience has been important to you and can be shared, but don't be surprised if each sentence you utter is broken up with words that give you a chance to pause. A countless number of remarks like "you know," "um," and similar phrases were omitted from the quotes of the women we interviewed. It's natural to be at a temporary loss for words. Have patience. You won't be denied access to communicating your aliveness. Inroads are made by listening and speaking to yourself and other women. Awkward speech is no reason to give up talking, any more than feeling clumsy justifies being inactive. Stay with it.

Forging ahead with verbal descriptions of a meaningful movement experience can lead to disappointment if the first time your listener misunderstands, you assume no one else can understand the significance of the experience. Several women said they had given up trying to share the experience after finding that the more they expressed themselves, the more the events seemed to be diminished. One or two bouts of unsuccessful communication was usually enough for these women to become unwilling to tell anyone else about their experiences.

One of these women was Wendy, who had had an exhilarating time cross-country skiing. "It takes away from the experience to try and tell people about it," she said, "because it can't, it won't ever be as exciting to somebody as it is to me, because I can still be there. I can still experience it. And to tell people about it takes away from its beauty because they don't feel the same way I do about it. No matter how much I verbalize it, or try to, other people weren't there and they can't feel the same wonder about it that I do. The few people that I tried to tell—it just took so much away from it that I don't tell many people about it anymore, except people that were there."

She explained what had been special: "It was new and exciting because I had done downhill before, but I'd never done cross-country, and I loved it. I loved being able to go out on ten feet of snow and know that I was ten feet up in the air, above the ground, and if I stepped off the skis, I would sink down over my head. And to be able to go uphill and down, and fast and slow and control it and go where I wanted to, where other people hadn't gone yet – fresh snow and making tracks, and all that. It was just an experience, plus it was a beautiful, beautiful place. The mountains and all."

She also described it as "the most beautiful picture you've ever seen, only it's real, and you're there in the middle of it, and you just want to stay forever. And I was there, and whenever I want to be there, I'm still there, in my head." What else does she recall? "All of it," Wendy said, "all the details, including taking off one ski and seeing if it was really that deep. Sticking my foot down and putting all my weight on my foot and going down to my hip on one leg, and having everybody pull me back out. And turning the ski over and sticking it down as far as we could and seeing how deep it was, and then pulling the ski back out. It's all still there."

Nothing says you must reveal to somebody else everything you do. But when you're about to burst with good feelings, try sprinkling your listener with drops of the experience rather than with a shower. If the other person is still interested, continue your story, keeping in mind that an empathetic listener needs some guidance to stay on track. Like Wendy, you're likely to have a detailed recollection of the movement experience. It takes some listening on your part, too, to be sure you're getting across what you think you are.

Knowing that the selfful experience really did happen and can't be taken away from you shows that communicating does not have to mean losing or giving up what is rightly yours. Support for valuing the selfful experience can also come when other people agree that what you felt is indeed worthwhile. Having teammates like Adele's who talked throughout the night or going skiing with a small group like Wendy did gives recognition to the experience when it happens.

Afterward, when the group splits up at the end of the season or vacation or time passes and old friendships dissolve, validating the movement experience may become more difficult. This is when women react by keeping the experience to themselves so it remains untarnished, rather than risking communicating with others. Cherishing the moment is fine. Suffocating it is not. Let it out. Voice your happiness. Ask a friend about her own experiences. Helping other women examine themselves as movers opens up new avenues of expression. The delights of moving are then more likely to be revealed than concealed.

7

Women in Motion:
New Images

INFORMATION IS easy to come by but difficult to assess accurately. Even with the availability of pamphlets, articles, television programs, and books, reaching for the most useful piece of information about women in motion may not come naturally. There are many sources, with different viewpoints, that can persuade and influence you. Deciding what you should take seriously is a step toward defining your active self.

The information in this book is no exception. Carefully weighing and digesting what is offered will be more helpful than swallowing everything whole. Trust your sense of questioning and suspicion. Just because something is packaged doesn't mean it's a gift you have to accept. See what makes sense to you. It's your opinion that counts.

The mass media constantly emit messages about active women. They also omit them. Think of your own life, your own experiences. Look at the movement activities you became aware of during the past week. You may have watched large groups of people who were moving or only noticed specific sports. Your role could have been as a participant, spectator, or both. Draw your recollections from the women you noticed, including yourself. Visualize risks, pathways, equipment, and tales. Keep looking. You'll remember many things.

Now divide everything you thought of into two categories: your own direct movement experiences and the indirect portrayal of women in motion by the mass media. There are, no doubt, discrepancies between the activities you do and those you see in the media. While you may have played racquetball, gone bicycling, or walked a nature trail, the media may have shown athletically skilled women competing at the national or international level. Through a filtering process, diversity is eliminated in media-portrayed activities. The product you see is polished and refined. You can only speculate about how a female athlete became skilled, what she thinks about while she's moving, and why she decided to make a career out of her activity. Such information is ignored or held back from the public. What you see, hear, and read about are women out to win – not necessarily women out to perform well.

What does this mean for you? Look at the standards you use to gauge your success. Although the activities you read about or watch on TV may be different from those you actually do, keeping score, traveling a certain distance, or counting wins and losses is likely central in what you do. Noting and keeping track of movement experiences probably isn't important. You haven't had access to information that depicts your life, so you use media standards as your own. If you go for a hike in the wilderness, how far you traveled may seem more important than what you saw or how you felt. If you meet a friend right after she has played a game of volleyball, you'll likely ask her who won.

Success is relative. There are many women who are successful at moving but don't know it. If the mass media are the only sources women use to verify success, they are doing themselves a disservice. They are unnecessarily restricting themselves to irrelevant standards. The number of women who are likely to imitate media women successfully is very small. Not all women make a career out of competing.

Most women have neither the skills nor the aspirations to become well-known female athletes. Doing as well as possible with occasional recognition is satisfying enough. What interferes with achieving this satisfaction is comparing oneself to media figures and not liking what one sees. The media restrict women's opinions of themselves as often as they provide usable role models.

Women see themselves in motion, and what they see is tempered by what they know of themselves and what they are told by others. When it comes to being active, it's no secret that women have yet to be applauded by society. Acceptance has grown, but there is still a long way to go. Because they must balance personal desires with social pressures, women view movement as less appealing than it really is.

To feel a sense of accomplishment and to find support and validation for that sense, women need somewhere to turn. Communications media are readily accessible, but they are weak as validators of movement experiences. It can be demoralizing to find nothing to compare oneself with. All the risks, pleasures, and novelties of being active may be pitted against a feeling of unrealness. If what you're doing is right, why is it so hard to find someone else with parallel experiences?

Taking mass media for what they're worth can provide relief and release. They contain bits and pieces of relevant information. Reading how more women are offered athletic scholarships or seeing women excel in a sport can offer encouragement. Knowing that being in motion isn't a dead-end venture is uplifting. Media can make women become aware of opportunities for moving. Professional women's teams have yet to reach their peak of popularity. Neighborhood recreation facilities attract only a small percentage of the women they can draw. As women find ways to act on their desires to move, mass media will be swayed to acknowledge the mass appeal of movement and its diversity of forms.

If you think you have to wait ten years before anything changes, think again. The mass media aren't the one-way channels they appear to be. Discussion can take place. There are publishers, directors, and editors who are responsible for the information you receive. Let these people know what it's like to be an active woman. Create an interest. Make the media come to you.

BLITZING MEDIA

Every woman has a story to tell. The mundane life of a mover can reveal at least one tale worth repeating. Although the audience you attract will differ in size and composition from that of the mass media, you have the right to express your experiences. To gain access to mass media, if you have something to tell the world, you need to know both what you want to say and how to present it. Think of yourself as a holder and seller of valuable information.

Some outlets are very easily overlooked. The world does not revolve around the TV evening news. During the day you come in contact with public service radio spots, weekly and daily newspapers, tabloids used for advertising or promoting specific opinions, cable TV channels that run printed messages of local concern across your TV screen, and many other forms of communication that vie for your attention. All of these are usable options for women to communicate about being in motion.

If you believe your daughter has fewer opportunities in athletics than do the boys at school; want to organize a fifty-and-older softball team but don't know enough women to get the idea off the ground; recently returned from a ski trip and have selfful experiences needing to be told, or want to find a partner to regularly work out with, you can use mass media to communicate your message.

To make the most of media, you have to know clearly what message you want to get across. Narrow down the idea until it is in its simplest and most direct form. Instead of saying "Some local girls are going to be at the school pool later on in the week to go against a rival school from across town," you can gather a following by saying "The girls' swim team is having an important meet on Saturday." In this way you create interest.

The same is true for high-caliber athletics. Highlight the importance of what you have to say. Get to the point before you lose your audience. "Our track team is expected to do well during the upcoming season" is bland when contrasted with "Two heavily recruited juniors are expected to set the pace for our best season yet." Given a piece of information, there are many ways to make it work – and then work even better. Isolate the heart of your message.

The way in which you present your information should be determined in part by your sense of your audience. To be effective, you need to recognize the type of audience the medium attracts as well as how the medium communicates to its audience. Are words central, or are visual images? Do you have five minutes to relay your message, or thirty seconds? The wonderful story you have about women being active will not get further than yourself if you don't consider these important things first. Remember, you have to interest the buyer in what you have to sell. Do some research before you try to tell your story through an inappropriate medium.

Within the medium or media you choose, there are individuals who won't give you the time of day, as well as avid listeners. If you are turned down by the sports department, speak with someone in news. If your favorite radio station is cordial but not interested, try another station. If you haven't been successful, use all the ties and contacts you can muster. A person working in the circulation department of a newspaper may be as helpful as the managing editor. Reporters acquire material for stories through many channels.

Regardless of who finally agrees to listen to you or look at your information, be organized. Have your thoughts and ideas in order before you pick up the telephone or walk out the door. This will make you an exception to the rule. Women who have a great sports tale to tell often place the burden of understanding and organizing on the listener. The woman who is quick, direct, and knowledgeable gains instant respect and attention. The same is true for a press release. You don't have to be a college or sports organization to have the right to issue a press release or public service announcement. When you do issue one, however, be sure it's clearly typed and lists the name, address, and phone number of a person to contact to verify the release or add more information. The less time someone else has to spend deciphering your message, the better off you are.

Do not overlook timing. A seminar on sports medicine for women will not be adequately covered by the media if it coincides with the season opener of a local major athletic event. To get the most coverage and attendance, check around town to avoid scheduling conflicts. Your local chamber of commerce, sports information offices at nearby colleges, and convention bureau can help keep you informed.

At times, local sporting events can be used to your advantage. You don't have to avoid them. A national tennis match can be used to point out the amateur competition and instruction available locally. A star soccer player who studies dance or the martial arts can lend credence to these programs in your town. Look for the twist that can tie media-accepted ideas to your own.

When you think about timing, don't forget deadlines. If you want to publicize an event that will occur at a specific time, waiting for the last minute will surely work against you. Sending releases out four weeks in advance isn't necessarily wise either. Give yourself a week and a half to two weeks. Most people don't eagerly run to a calendar to write down a time and place; they use their memories. If you're not sure what timing will work best, ask the media you're targeting. They'll give you their advice and policies.

After the event, go immediately to the telephone or typewriter. Old news is no news. Report the information while it's fresh and of interest. Consider:

- Can I supply a photograph with the story?
- Do I have people's names correctly spelled?
- Is there a night telephone number that's different from the regular number?
- How can the information be relayed with the broadest appeal possible?

- Is there an upcoming event the media would be interested in knowing about and covering?

Operating with advanced planning works in your favor. You may even discover media that will accept collect calls if you make prior arrangements.

The more active you are in using media, the more comfortable you become in finding outlets for your stories. As your involvement increases, your awareness changes. Information about active women has a suitable place in the media. Perseverance pays off. Column inches and air time suddenly appear when you believe in the information you're offering and remain determined to locate an individual media representative who will listen.

Invite a reporter or sportscaster to take a firsthand look at what you're doing. Supply the times you expect to start and end. If that request is turned down, ask that a photographer be sent. There are always more options than you think there are.

Women in motion offer many stories and angles to attract the communications media. Increasing your identification and dissemination of worthy news will increase the coverage. Be proud. You've sold someone else on a product you've been sold on for a long time.

To secure a voice for yourself and other women, put yourself in an influential position. Imagine *you* are the sports editor for the local newspaper. You are not new to journalism; you've always been a reporter. Now you're responsible for assigning and editing the stories. Suddenly you realize that to ensure the high circulation the newspaper boasts, you have to appeal to a wide range of readers. Your personal view is only one of many. As a woman who is athletically active, you want to support other women by providing coverage whenever possible. After four weeks on the job, the most you've been able to print is an announcement of an upcoming girls' gymnastics camp. You know that other activities must be going on, but you never hear about them. Nobody has bothered to inform you.

In the meantime, coaches, athletes, and parents have kept the phones ringing about high school football. Everyone is pleased about the articles that have appeared. There are more than enough stories. In fact, you're working with your display advertising staff in preparation for a football supplement soon to come out.

Given your commitment to active women, your role as a sports editor, and the spare time you barely have, you

- hold off on the advertising supplement until you can include women in it other than cheerleaders;
- go on with the job as is and hope someone will send more notices and announcements about girls and women in motion;
- don't think twice about making changes in the sports and activities covered;
- publish an editorial requesting that readers submit ideas on ways to expand the focus of the sports section; or
- assign a reporter to do an article on the gymnastics camp.

What would you do?

Media weigh diversity against practicality. Expanding the scope of coverage may be seen as an unnecessary risk. In other words, media are reluctant to change a good thing; they'd rather stay with what has worked in the past. As consumers of information, women need to understand this viewpoint. The media you approach with your message or story may automatically shy away from acting on your request. Risks are as real to media as they are to individuals.

Don't back off. Keep this in mind when you phone in a story or mail in an announcement, and do what you can to make your message a part of the usual flow of information in that newspaper, TV program, or radio show. Women in motion are natural to you. Use descriptions to make them appear natural to someone else as well.

New information can come across as threatening. Present your news items in a familiar context. Make your listener feel at home. Local media strive to do the same thing. They reflect community events. People you know or know of turn up on a page or screen. By localizing and personalizing information, media get your attention. Capitalize on this. Tell the local media you want more publicity for the girls' soccer team you coach. You know the girls are giving their all, yet they never make it onto the sports pages.

Use a personal approach. Speak with the sports editor personally. Go armed with supportive data. Know how many girls and parents are represented in the soccer league. Emphasize community ties. Any unusual angles, such as the following, will also work in your favor:

- Sisters who are on opposing teams
- Players with skills or maneuvers that set them apart from the others
- Experiences the girls became excited about
- Girls who overcame a fear of the sport
- How coaches became interested in the job
- Different skills players can master

Also know the type of coverage you would prefer and what you would accept. An annual feature may satisfy everyone, or maybe highlights of each game are important to you. A weekly soccer column or report during the season can help your girls as players and the readers as spectators. Are you able and willing to write one, or do you want the newspaper or TV station to be responsible?

If you are still overlooked, ignored, or told "I'd write a story, but no one would read it," ask your players to write to the editor of the newspaper or the producer of the TV show . Another alternative is to seek out the living section editor, which used to be called the women's section. This isn't a step down. It's a step across. If your aim is publicity, try to get information into the news part of the newspaper. Anyone can buy a classified advertisement. Everyone can't maneuver her way under a by-line or into a photo. Compromising is a pact with reason. Get your foot in the door. Later you can choose whether you prefer it to be your left or your right foot.

In whatever way your voice is projected, get as close as you can to telling your own story. Let the girls on the soccer team be quoted. Draw the parents into an interview. Add the voices of spectators and officials to your own. Make the situation come alive.

UNSCRAMBLING MESSAGES

Media-portrayed women have mixed images. They are active and competitive, and they take their involvement seriously. On the other hand, they are composed, sleek, and feminine. If a racket is thrown or an obscenity uttered, the individual is held accountable, not the sex.

On the surface it seems that media approve of women in motion. Looking closer you may find that many women are omitted from the scope of acceptability. A woman with a few extra pounds of fat doesn't fit the mold. Women's achievements are lowered a notch by comparisons with men's records. When women and men have a dual meet, men are usually called men, and women are called ladies. It is very difficult for active women to be successful in the media's eyes.

Increasing the accuracy of women's role in movement is a must if all women are to envision and act on their own styles of personal fitness. Messages from media and individuals have to be divided into truth and hot air. Analyzing the messages you receive is a way of discovering what's really being said.

The fitness fad has popularized exercise for women. The impression is that women are all right if they choose to be active, but the picture lacks images of sweaty, non-leotarded, older, and diverse women. Even as muscles are becoming in vogue, they are still attached to bodies resembling models'. Strength is played down. Sexiness is played up.

Mixed messages like these are easily overlooked. At first glance, they seem to support women. On a closer look, however, you can see that they support only certain types of women. Fatigued, out-of-breath, disheveled women are rarely seen or mentioned. An example is a regular feature on a TV network. For a few minutes, a woman does aerobic exercises. With music in the background, the TV figure exercises nonstop. Supposedly, the women in the audience are to join in. If you really want to follow along, by the time you figure out what the woman is doing, the show is at least half over. The TV cameras offer no help. They follow only the woman's breasts, crotch, and buttocks. The message that exercise is fitting for women is mixed with the message that women are sexual objects when they move.

Lost in the accuracies of depicting moving women are the aesthetics of the moment. Watching movement is seeing beauty come alive. Muscles tense, joints flex, and limbs move through space. The artful complement of mover and surroundings is second to none. Each movement is slightly different from the next. No one is ever sure what the following moment will reveal. To view women in motion this way is to witness the heart of human movement. Focusing on the essence of animation is a given right for everyone. Taking the time and initiative to experience motion leads to an appreciation of other people moving.

The focus on who's ahead, how someone can be beaten, or how far an object can be thrown limits the message. There's nothing original to say. The time, the place, and the players differ from one situation to the next, but those can be plugged into simple sentences and endlessly repeated. Expressing the uniqueness of movement takes more effort. Many more messages and ideas must be conveyed to capture pure movement. For some the uniqueness lies in the way a skier swiftly passes over snow. To others it is in their own stop-action as a football touches a receiver's hands. Motion is instantaneous and infinite.

To unscramble messages, see what you want to see regardless of what an announcer is saying or a camera is focused on. Pick out what interests you and become your own producer, publisher, or editor. Show yourself what motion is like. Pleasing yourself is paramount. You need not confuse your pleasures with contradictory messages. Experiencing movement makes you an expert.

Examine the information you receive from all sources. Be aware of the language and expressions you use as well. You transmit as well as receive. Everyone shares a responsibility for accuracy and for making valid interpretations.

Sift through the information you have. Remember that what is represented in the media is a limited representation of women in motion. No matter how many programs, books, or articles there are, there will always be another way to view the information. Keep looking, until you are satisfied.

VOICING YOUR VIEWS BY NETWORKING

The mass media offer one avenue of expression. Active women can transmit messages in other ways. Posters, informal newsletters, and an exchange of journal or diary entries are other options. Word of mouth is very effective and satisfying too.

Communicating person to person on a regular basis may become as important to you as any activity you engage in. It makes everything you do more real. Try to meet people who understand muscle pulls, game strategy, and the latest equipment. Take someone along with you when you engage in your activity to show why you like being active. Let the person know what you think about before, during, and after your performance. Welcome people. Reinforce your natural connection with daily movement experiences.

In this way you begin forming your own support networks, enabling you to exchange information, find new partners, share driving expenses to and from outlying facilities, and get to know what other women are thinking and doing. Discuss your running shoes and how they wear or hold up. Give your opinion on the value of the different clubs in town. Verbalize how you like to move and how you don't. Share your fears and embarrassments, as well as your hints about your activity.

Each woman needs to speak with other women and speak for herself. Learn to describe yourself in motion through your own words. Become aware of your body, what you look like, how you feel. Notice other moving women. Express how they appear to you. Interact with them by sharing your observations. The joys of movement can be locked inside unsaid words. Through verbalization, you begin to hear the role that movement plays in your life. You discover what you've done and can do. Words free ideas. Relating to movement isn't foreign.

There's no telling what life would be like if all the active women who keep their thoughts to themselves got together to communicate. Establishing a network of vocal women would lend support to beginners as well as experienced movers. Making connections would allow women to approach each other with fears, joys, and concerns. With an outlet for expressing their experiences, women could feel secure about being in motion. Without a voice, women have no power. Even if they do have an opinion, no one will know it — maybe not even themselves.

Take a look at your vocabulary. Is it sufficient, or does it need to be expanded? Words like *defeat, win, victor, loser, second-string, starter, record,* and *captain* are limiting. They describe some, but not all, situations. Women can also treat themselves to words like *satisfying, fun, challenging, invigorating, play, strategy, self-testing,* and *different.* For a rounded view, don't leave out *breathless, sweaty, tired, sore,* and *done.*

To test out your vocabulary, watch a woman moving. Say to yourself what she's doing. If you quickly run out of descriptive words, focus on her face. Then describe the flow of her movement. Does she cover much ground, move quickly, hesitate, interact with people around her, or seem involved in what she's doing? A picture of moving women is much more complete when scoreboards take a secondary role.

Pick a memory of yourself moving. In whatever ways you've verbalized the scene before, try different words and phrases. Look at yourself from twenty feet above. Take the perspective of someone else who may have been watching you. Your own eyes may see the situation in a new light or from a different direction.

8
A Personal Conclusion

WE HAVE ASKED one another to describe our lives in motion. We have highlighted more than our day-to-day experiences, collecting short accounts of our involvement with movement and pointing out what we'd like to see or change. This is something we ask each of you to do, and it's only fair that we do the same.

DAPHNE

When I think about all the movement activities I enjoy, I find one common thread. Somewhere within each activity is the possibility for a moment of joyous glory when nothing matters except the sensations of the moment. During these times, I do things I advise others not to do. I show that I've swallowed the traditional competitive sport ethic.

I played on a rugby team for about six months. I would have played longer, but my moment of glory cut my time short. I met it head on and ended up with my knee in a cast. There was a loose ball on the ground between me and an opposing player. We were both determined to kick it, and we reached it simultaneously. As we kicked, her knee slammed into mine. I had to be carried from the field right then, but I returned to the game after twenty minutes with barely a second thought. Two days later, a visit to an orthopedist proved I had had no business returning to the field.

I've seen that happen time and again, from informal street games to the Olympic arena. A player becomes injured and before she has a chance to be fully healed or even thoroughly examined, she is back in the game. The injury could be anything from abrasions to broken bones. The decision to continue playing may be shared by the player and her coach, athletic trainer, or doctor. Consideration may be given to the type and severity of the injury, the nature of the game, the player's desire to return, and the player's importance to the team's performance.

If the woman continues to play, measures may be taken to reduce the chance of further injury. The injured part may be protected in some way or the player given a less vulnerable position. On the other hand, precautions may not be taken at all. She may even be given a painkiller to help her ignore the injury, thus making her more susceptible to further injury.

I would like to see women take a leadership role in this area of safety and sanity in movement activities. I want to learn to be more aware of the attitudes in myself and in my culture that make me willing to sacrifice my health and safety.

Many of the problems I see involve team sports. The opportunities available to women are usually organized around which team is best. The emphasis on win-lose records, league standings, and championships attests to such an attitude. Because of this, teams tend to put only their best players on the court or field, even if these players happen to be sick or injured.

Some organizations seek to alleviate the problem by separating stronger and weaker teams, but this still does nothing for women who don't wish to be a part of a league at all or who rarely make it to the starting line-up. What about women who want to play just for fun?

Sports and movement participation by nonexperts and beginners is important. Each woman is a beginner in some area. Learning to gain competence in an activity has thrills that are no less exciting than those of performing well at a mastered task. Women of all skill levels deserve opportunities for moments of joyous glory – or selfful experiences.

The traditional view of movement activities, based on winning and losing, seems to limit participation rather than expand it. Every woman has heard the trite pronouncements about the importance of winning. Other things feel better to me than winning the game, however. One of them is knowing I'm doing my best and having that feeling further enhanced by knowing that others, on *both* teams, are also doing their best. At times, this striving melts into an ease of communication that is highly nonverbal and intuitive, and the whole team works as a unit. That feels better than winning any day.

Winning against a good team in a game that was well played by both teams feels especially good. But so does losing in the same situation. What I find particularly troublesome is the winning person or team that gloats and puts the other team down by its attitude of superiority and the losing team that is full of excuses. Rugby teams have a tradition that seeks to erase these reactions. After every game, the teams party together to celebrate the joy of playing. A team's party reputation is usually as well known as its playing ability.

Even though winners don't have to gloat and losers don't have to pout, I would like to see more ways to engage in movement activities that lessen or eliminate the focus on competition. One way is to de-emphasize the role of the referee or umpire. The traditional system of rule enforcement seems to have increased the amount of roughness and violence that players are willing to use to win. When outside rule enforcers are present, players get the subtle, indirect message that they are not responsible for their own behavior. The officials must control the game yet simultaneously not interfere with its flow. That's a very thin tightrope to walk on. Achieving consistency from situation to situation is very difficult. Somehow, the presence of officials has encouraged the philosophy that it's all right to do anything as long as you don't get caught.

Sadly, as players give away their responsibility in this way, they are also giving away their power to create the playing situation they desire. If the situation seems to require more or less leniency, for example, the players cannot make that happen. If one team wants to handicap itself in some way, that is not allowed. In many activities, the individual herself would know if she had broken a rule, and she could simply say so. In some instances, other players, both teammates and opponents, would be in a position to make a judgment. Sometimes a brief discussion among players would be the best way to arrive at a fair decision.

I can imagine a volleyball game in which any player on the court calls net fouls or a softball game in which players from the batting team take turns being the umpire behind the plate. "I can imagine that too," you might be saying. "There would be utter chaos with endless arguments." That might be true, or it might not. If women wanted to try this option for game playing, procedures for settling disagreements would evolve in the spirit of players' personal responsibility for their play. Rules would probably be amended or replaced.

Another way to focus on the joy of movement instead of on winning would be to organize events for individuals, pairs, or teams that put more emphasis on working together than on having winners and losers. Incorporating every player into the action would be stressed. I can envision a new kind of soccer game in which each team has its own ball that must be moved through five or seven wickets placed at different parts of the field as in croquet, but not in ordered sequence. The wickets would be only twice the size of the ball, and only a single player in control of the ball could approach within a six-foot radius. No one could guard her there. Also, a different player from the team would send the ball through each wicket. All of this would be done while trying to prevent the opposing team from doing the same thing.

For individuals or pairs, I would like to see events organized in ways that allow everyone to succeed. My fantasy for myself would be a new kind of running event, one that's interspersed with surprise activities and ways of covering distance other than running. Some of the things to include would be running on trails, jumping over branches, rolling down grassy hills, walking on logs, wading or swimming through water, crawling through a cave, climbing up and down a tree, rock-hopping, traveling on a rope bridge, or paddling a canoe. It's the same idea as an obstacle course, but using as many natural obstacles as possible for fun and challenge.

The surprise events could even be designed so that the cooperation of a partner is necessary, and pairs of women would do the course together. Instead of starting together at the same spot and trying to be the first to finish, women could start simultaneously at different parts of the course or start from the beginning every twenty seconds or so. This way it would be harder to compare oneself with others, and it might be easier to focus on the movement and what it means in a more personal sense. Emphasis would be on enjoyment and self-challenge rather than speed alone, though women could run at any speed they wanted. There might even be ways for a woman to vary her route if she wanted to, choosing her own level of challenge.

As I've been suggesting ways that movement activities might be more meaningful to women, I realize I'm about to fall into another bad habit of mine. Sometimes I get the notion that everyone views or experiences a situation the same way I do. It's not that I feel other people's views and feelings are wrong, it's just that I haven't taken time to find out what they are before offering mine.

When I'm taking the role of leader, whether as a writer or on a backpacking expedition, this bad habit causes women to enjoy movement less instead of more. While I really want women to explore options and create new structures, I lessen that possibility by imposing my own values and ideas without taking enough time to listen.

Once when I taught a backpacking course and organized a trip for the women involved, I carefully chose a trail that was very gradual except for one steep part in the middle. What I failed to consider was that the six or eight narrow log bridges we had to use to cross over streams would not highlight the trip for anyone but me.

Although my group didn't tell me until later (because I didn't ask), every other backpacker would have preferred a route without that particular challenge. I had also made some other incorrect assumptions. Those women helped me learn a very valuable lesson. I'm glad I had a chance to evaluate the trip with them afterward and that they were honest with me about their feelings.

After all the suggestions I've made, I wouldn't want you to feel bad because you don't live up to your own ideal of a woman in motion. I don't always do what I know is good for me either. It's not that easy and I know it! I have not yet solved all the problems of integrating my favorite and most meaningful activities into my daily life while dealing with responsibilities to work, home, and other people. All I can do is be aware of what I want and try to find a balance of what works best.

Running is a perfect example. I like to run, both sprints and distances. I can run near my house or my place of work, and I have at least a couple of friends who will run with me. I can take the dogs with me to places not too far away and alleviate some of the guilt I feel that they don't get to run enough. This pleases me and also meets one of my home responsibilities. Running also relaxes me and helps me sleep well at night. If I run regularly, I can eat as much as I want without gaining weight.

Even with all of that going for me, however, I still go for months at a time without running. I wear my running shoes a lot, and I think about running almost every day. Still, I choose not to run because I'd rather sleep late, it's raining, it's hot, I don't feel like changing clothes, or any other excuse. I feel guilty when I don't run, but that's still not enough to make me run.

What's the magic key? What's so different about the times when I do run regularly? There seem to be two situations that help me to include running in my life on a routine basis. One is when I have a goal to reach, such as being in shape for backpacking or being ready to run a race I've already committed myself to. These goals are usually a type of outside motivator that I take advantage of.

The other is more internally motivated. I make time for running simply because it's a nice thing to do for myself. Sometimes I am more certain than at other times that it's just as important to take care of my own needs and desires as it is to meet my responsibilities to others. I am trying to do this more often, but I haven't yet learned to do it all the time.

My best strategy seems to be to combine the internal and external motivators. Knowing how much I enjoy backpacking, for instance, I make reservations for a wilderness permit or promise to take others on a trip. Then, with the date of the expedition firmly fixed, I start running regularly so I will be in shape when the trip comes. While I'm running, I enjoy thinking about the upcoming trip and previous ones too.

I hope someday to be totally spontaneous about participating in the movement activities that are important to me and not to play such games with myself. I may even find that the times I choose not to move are important in ways I've yet to understand. A few of the puzzle pieces have begun to fall into place. I hope you will also discover ways to pull together your needs and desires relating to movement.

PAT

People assume because I'm grounded in the area of sports and fitness that a lifetime of fitness comes easily for me. It does not. What comes easily is helping others enter the world of movement, explore their movement options, or expand on their current activities. When it comes to myself, however, I go through agonizing crises trying to fit exercise into my own routine. In spite of my background, it's difficult for fitness to be an integral part of my life.

After years of having sport and play facilities at my fingertips because of my profession, I took movement for granted. It was something that just happened. I didn't need to plan for it. Now I have had to acquire the necessary skills and motivation to move regularly without the luxuries of easily accessible facilities and the flexibility of time. This does take planning.

This book has forced me to think about how infrequently I move and why. I am a goal-oriented person and have set goals for myself in every other area of my life – except movement needs. By neglecting to set movement goals, I am more apt to engage in activities in a very halfhearted, random fashion with no real commitment or direction.

A hard, honest look at my priorities has brought certain things to light. I keep placing everything else before my movement needs. I love to move, but doing something so enjoyable strictly for me seemed selfish. But I'm changing. Recently, when my children were home on vacation, I chose to go to my aerobic dance class. I felt I needed it and really wanted to go, for me. It meant finding a ride for my daughter to attend a skating party, a sitter for my son, and a ride to dance class for myself. I did it – and came home feeling great. At one point I would have said the heck with it and sat home harboring ill feelings and resenting my family for not letting me do what I wanted. It has taken me a while to be honest and to realize I have been the only person stopping myself.

I'm a competitor and I still have trouble doing something just for the sake of doing it. I don't jog, I sprint. I don't dance without trying to kick my legs higher than anyone else or make my movements more vigorous. I race through life just as I race through activities. This intensity with which I choose to perform is hard to sustain. To perform at that level every time is not possible, and it often leaves me feeling inadequate or not up to par. Movement forms without this element of competition are good for me, allowing me to become more involved in the movement itself and not get caught up in competition. They give me more of a chance to participate.

I find downhill skiing suitably noncompetitive. It's a very freeing experience. There's no competition with anyone. Just woman against the mountain and the elements. I love to ski fast, trying to adeptly handle unexpected moguls, changes in terrain and snow conditions, as well as the steepness of the slopes. It's challenging yet great fun to feel the wind on my face, hear the rush of my skis over the snow, and take in the glorious panorama of snow-covered mountains. It satisfies my needs for adventure, beauty, and exercise.

Communicating through movement brings enjoyment to me, too. I have an acquaintance to whom I do not relate well verbally. We seem to have little in common, and we disagree about whatever we discuss. But on the tennis court, it's another story. We play beautifully as a doubles team. The court is the one place where I know exactly what she's thinking, her strengths, weaknesses, and the type of game she likes to play. I cover for her weaknesses and help her to use her strengths. She does the same for me. We communicate and tune into each other beautifully through that activity. We have found a common ground that binds us and have found a new respect and appreciation for each other.

Communication works in other ways too. Mary and I interact well verbally. We're frenetic when we're together. Our physical activity and our mouths never quit. We burn each other out. Sometimes I try to avoid her when I'm too tired to interact at such a high level. Now we take a dance class together. The music plays instead of our mouths, and we relax and communicate with our movements. We enjoy each other more now, for we've learned how to be together in a more relaxed setting. The ability to help one another gear down and give new direction to our energy has been added to our relationship.

In the future, besides finding other ways to be communicative, I'd like it to be common and natural for women to engage in a predinner game of basketball or a morning stretch. It would be easy for mother and daughter, sisters, friends, and roommates to enjoy hours of regular activity without being labeled jock, selfish, negligent mother, immature, or lesbian.

I would like to see movement as a priority in women's lives, with women participating in their own movement forms and not just what is socially acceptable. Everyone would be able to participate without feeling guilty or arousing feelings of resentment in others. Families would be active, either together or separately, but all sharing the joy of movement.

In my own family background, I still have not adjusted to the differential treatment my sister and I received. I participated on many teams in a variety of sports throughout my childhood and college years. I don't recall my parents coming to see me once in all those years. But they went to the men's basketball games and the men's football games. They cheered for them. But they did not do the same for my sister and me. We always had their support, in a passive way. The active involvement was directed to the men.

This attitude still bothers me today. We see it in the scheduling of women's games. Women's games are pregames — prior to the men's events. We still see parents who do not support the girls in their family the way they do the boys — to go see them, to cheer, to give that active support, to get as emotionally involved with their daughters as they do with their sons.

Women are playing at the same level. It means as much to us as it does to the men. I feel that by observing on two different levels, spectators put males and females on two different levels. I'm still adjusting to this fact that we are not taken seriously. It's an adjustment I've been making my whole life. My parents obviously thought it was fine for me to do what I did, but it wasn't worthy of active or emotional support. I'm trying very hard with my own children not to do that. It's hard because my daughter, Kendra, is active in feminine, acceptable types of movement, gymnastics and ballet. That's where her strengths lie. But I try my hardest to give her the same emotional support as I do my son, Todd. My husband and I do become more involved in Todd's activities. We cheer when we want Todd and his teammates to score a soccer goal or when someone hits a home run. Gymnastics and ballet classes for preschoolers and youngsters do not lend themselves to this type of spectatorship. I've often wondered if I'm just using the fact that Kendra is gifted in these areas as an excuse, that the activities I put her in are restricted to those that our society considers appropriate for girls. I'm not sure there isn't already a built-in bias with me.

It's very hard to break away from that. You tend to do to your children what was done to you. I think almost unconsciously I am doing to Kendra what my parents did to me. Maybe she wants to be part of a team and hear us yell, "C'mon Kendra. You can score. You can make a goal!" or "You can hit a home run" or "C'mon – steal second!" We've never done that with her. She has always been in activities that did not warrant the type of cheering we have done for Todd.

From some of her comments, I feel she misses it. She has already perceived at age six that we cheer for and engage in sports with Todd on a totally different level. We've had to do some soul-searching as parents. Granted, she is interested in and good at activities that are not team-oriented. But I really owe it to her to give her the chance to get the adulation, the claps, the pats on the behind, and the "Hey, give me five." She should experience that. She very much wants to have the same experiences as her brother.

I think that's something we as women and mothers adjust to constantly. Just think about what types of activities you put your daughters in, and think about what you put your sons in. I know that I enjoyed all the applause and all ten spectators at my games. I enjoyed all the pats and the thrill of scoring a basket or a goal. It meant a lot to me. But I've had to adjust to not getting the same respect and the same level of spectatorship as the men. I'm trying not to perpetuate this practice in the rearing of my daughter.

As parents, we expect more of our sons than we do of our daughters. We expect them to participate on a different level. It even shows up sometimes in the way we dress our children. Our daughter goes in matching shorts and shirt to practice. Our son wears a ripped-up shirt and dirty pants. He's very masculine. He's all boy. Our daughter would be perfectly happy wearing an ugly old T-shirt that was passed on from three other people and a pair of her brother's rotten old gym shorts. Mom is the one who would be uncomfortable. And Mom passes on that prejudice and bias. It's okay for my daughter to do what my son does as long as she looks like a little girl. Well, that's not fair.

When I think of the role models I had when growing up, the women always wore beautiful little puffy, velour, velvet-type exercise outfits. I never saw pictures of them sweating, grunting, groaning, or working hard. It was made to look very glamorous. That has affected my life. I don't mind sweating. I don't mind working hard. But I always try to make sure that when I am, I still retain my femininity. My hair isn't wet, stringy, and disheveled, I still have some makeup on, and I'm not dressed in well-worn shorts and old sweats. Through my appearance I'm trying to make the social comment that I can play and be physically active in socially unacceptable activities while I'm still a good wife, a good mother, and a mature woman.

Athletics was and still is my ticket to being accepted by others. Some women choose drama. Some choose music. Because I was good at athletics and I knew I would be wanted on teams, I used sports. I think even to this day I use it. Most of the women my age are not as active, fit, enthusiastic, or involved as I am in life. I still try to play tennis and volleyball weekly and go to aerobic dance classes three times a week. I enjoy the recognition and the obvious approval I get from people, male and female.

I'm close to forty and people expect me to be oiling up the wheelchair. Instead, on a good day, I can fit in thirty-six hours of work and play into twenty-four hours. I attribute a lot of that to exercise and the fact that I can release a lot of tension and anxiety through movement and sport. In the process, I do something for my body, and it shows. I'm almost forty going on eighteen. I wish all women could feel this way.

SANDY

Both Daphne and Pat have performed, so it's my turn to do what I like to do in movement activities—be in the anchor

position to wrap things up. Having these pressures and responsibilities are ways of competing with myself. A challenging task requires concentration to be done well.

When I'm down two games in tennis or I need at least a
strike or a spare to bowl my average or a score I'm after, a
world of possibilities opens up. I see new places to serve to
and different ways to release the bowling ball. Instead of
narrowing down my options, I think of how many ways I can
achieve my goal.

If my serves don't go in or the pins don't go down, I'm disappointed but not devastated. I handle this disappointment
in one of two ways. Either I feel strong and secure about
having done what I could or I become annoyed at myself and
question how I could have possibly done what I did. I'm still
learning how to look at my performance, not just my expectations. There's always something I can feel good about if I
replay the whole process—my footwork, intentions, position—in addition to the result.

This isn't always easy. One incident that happened at least
ten years ago still affects me. I loved volleyball, so I signed
up for a class. Power volleyball had just become popular, so I
had to learn a new style of playing. As part of my evaluation,
I had to hit the volleyball into the floor and make it rebound
close to the gym's ceiling. I couldn't do it. I used all my
strength and know-how and still couldn't get that ball to do
what I wanted it to do. The instructor was more disbelieving
than I was. No instructions were able to translate how to succeed at the task. I still have a distaste for volleyball.

Several years before that, I was taking a fitness test. By
performing above a certain percentile on each task, I would
be one of the deserving recipients of a special award. Duly
motivated, I went all-out—which turned out to be not
enough. I couldn't go the distance in the standing broad
jump. All those other great scores meant nothing. I didn't
earn the award.

If I got stuck on moments like these, I'd be content to
watch television and pop cookies into my mouth. But I'm

driven by something else. I have an urge to do something. To be active. To be and stay in motion.

As a youngster, I loved to jump up. As a consequence, I came down. I'd joyfully jump and reach as high as I could in the house, going for a covered beam or the ceiling. Time and time again I'd fingerprint my way to the upper reaches of the house and crash down to a destined landing. All was well unless my marks on the walls were spotted or the apartment dwellers below noticed their light fixture swinging.

I still have the same urges, but I don't act on them as often. I let the social consequences spoil some of my fun. That's not saying I don't surprise anyone, myself included. I haven't given up. I'm just more subtle.

Moving is fun. It's a pleasure. The one week I had to use crutches was enough to remind me how active I normally am. I had no idea how much motion it took to drop a letter by the post office; do my weekly food shopping; push in on the clutch of my car; walk up the short, steep grade in front of the house; get up a flight of stairs; or be comfortable in bed. I know now.

I also know what it's like to feel the weight of inactivity. It doesn't feel right. It's a burden. But at least I'm familiar enough with that feeling to do something about it. Being able to change the weight of inactivity to the gravity-challenging prospect of being in motion is very appealing. I'm addicted to running around; tying myself into shoes of different sports; playing in baggy-kneed cotton sweats; balancing on the edges of curbs; and using an assortment of rackets. The movement and the equipment have me mesmerized. I'm in motion for life.

If all the sports known to women were to disappear today, I'd be at a loss – but only temporarily. I know I like to use my upper body, especially my hands. As long as my hands had a central part to play, I'd be happy. My legs and feet add the harmony. They keep me going and in balance as my upper body performs the intricate movements. I hit a discord when the central roles are switched. It's just not the same.

So I know what I do well, but I'm not pleased. I have an elusive sensation that I've narrowed my vision. I've let racket sports take over as my choices. What happened to volleyball, basketball, and softball? Why haven't I found a way to be out folk dancing? I don't know, but I can speculate. I'm a singles player. Any activity where the outcome is based on what I do is attractive. Being a part of a group with a common goal bores me. There's always something else I'd prefer to do. By myself, I can try new things without worrying about how the group will be affected. My individual performance is monitored by one person – me.

There are exceptions. I'll play in a foursome in golf, or doubles in a racket sport, or a group game if the other players have a spirit of fun and adventure. I don't want to be manipulated by other people who want me to play a certain type of game. My version of serious and intense is not one in which any incorrect move is a mistake. I avoid people who have reactions like this.

No matter how much I want to do well or win, I still want to enjoy what I'm doing. That's as true for badminton as it is for backpacking. I'll take the risks on my own terms – self-satisfaction using my own standards.

As for folk dancing, performing or learning in a group is just about the same to me. I value the complexity of matching my own abilities to a situation more than I do adjusting myself to a group. Concentrating on the bowling pin left standing or the open space my opponent has left on a tennis court is more important to me than blending with a group. The challenge is in meeting situations, not in adjusting to people.

People create the situations. If women weren't in motion, nothing would happen. But when women are in motion, the unexpected is likely to occur. Simply because I'm unable to

forecast events when I'm active, I'm drawn to movement.
Given all my experiences, I can only guess the outcome and
what will happen along the way.

Whenever I start thinking my movement repertoire isn't
broad enough, I think of a young child. She can spend an endless amount of time playing with a rubber ball. Once the ball
or the child moves ever so slightly, magically the whole universe looks different to the child. The ball and the child are
forever in motion. There's excitement and mystery. I want
each situation to be like that. Whatever is going on, I want to
be able to grasp what's unique.

Once when Daphne, Pat, and I were working together, we
were temporarily sidetracked. How it started I don't know,
but for the better part of an hour the three of us spontan-
eously patted, smashed, kicked, ran after, stretched for, and
elbowed two helium-filled balloons. At times the unspoken
objective was to keep the balloons from touching the floor,
while at other times the aim was to try to place the balloons
just out of reach or past someone.

If I had been invited to hit balloons around for an hour in
an area of less than one hundred square feet, I would have
wondered if I had heard right. But all the pieces fell into place
for the three of us to be uninhibited and act on what we were
writing about. Two balloons and three women became an ad-
venturesome mixture.

No matter how excited and boisterous I get, though, I'm
still aware that everyone doesn't share my enthusiasm. I
have friends who think playing racquetball in such an
enclosed area is a death wish, and others who get a distant
look when I talk about an activity I've done. On one level, I'd
probably like everyone to treasure the pleasures of being in
motion. On another, I know I place the significance of movement at a very special level. Everyone else isn't obligated to
do likewise.

Maybe there's a touch of selfishness, but if more women
don't continue being active and enjoying it, then who am I
going to be able to play with twenty, thirty, or forty years

from now? Pitching horseshoes is fine, but I do want some human interaction. What's the fun of slicing a golf ball and having it rebound off two trees if there's no one there to share it with? How am I going to develop and try out new activities if no one else wants to play?

I could use a few good role models, too. I've been lucky to have been around many skilled female athletes, but the women with a spirit of play have been rarer. Finding women who combine the two has not happened often either. Daring to duel with risks and challenges is more meaningful to me than staying within the confines of rules. Who will show me and other women what else is possible? How can we influence one another?

The more I sense what can be, the happier I get. Selfful experiences and special moments are just glimpses of what interaction can be like. The nonverbal channels women have yet to open up are not too far away. Motion lends itself to experiences of the senses. Communication fits right in.

Knowing the ball will be thrown to you, or the person you're guarding will be shifting to the left, or the arrow will hit the target precisely where it's aimed, or the shuttlecock will stay in play although it looks as if it will be out, are situations taken for granted. Intuition and experience play a part. They're glued together with nonverbal communication. The message has reached you. Where did it come from? Why is it so accurate? Nonverbal channels offer an untapped wealth of possibilities for women in motion.

Becoming aware of movement all around you brings a taste of what is already going on. Running out of things to do isn't likely if you and other women remain active. Take a close look at yourself. I do. I see who has influenced me and what impressions I've made on others. I know how my enthusiasm for enjoyable movement spreads to anyone around me. Someone, somewhere helped me. You can do the same – for yourself.

Acknowledging that moving feels right can make any experience that much better. Women need to see how moving is vital to living and how these special movement experiences ripple and flow throughout their lives. Staying attached to the moment enlivens each experience. Willfully moving yields plenty of self-satisfaction.

Simple, almost forgettable moments make up most of your movement experiences. Mixed in are more reasons to stay active. Braving the elements, trying a new variation of a skill, becoming aware of footwork, feeling coordinated, not throwing a temper tantrum when you lose, and finally having pieces fall into place are valuable and special experiences that are earthshaking in their own way.

Looking at and reviewing any segment of yourself in motion will reveal these special times. Find out what they are and make them more apparent. Go into the activity knowing you will be able to get something out of it. Be intense. Be humorous. Be yourself.

And if you catch yourself unable to utter a single pleasantry about being a moving woman, think again. You have had the chance to have selfful experiences and special moments. Enjoy the recollections and the movement experiences yet to come.

Sandy Hayden, Daphne Hall, and Pat Stueck are coach/trainers for whom being in motion is a way of life. Hayden, former women's sports information director at the University of Arkansas, Fayetteville, has written about women and sports for the *Greensboro Daily News* and the *Northwest Arkansas Times*. Hall provides movement experiences for children ages two through nine in her classes, "Kids in Motion," and has written on sports for the *Athens Observer*. Stueck, former New England Director of Women's Athletics for the National Junior College Athletic Association, specializes in teaching adult fitness. All three live in Athens, Georgia.